Winning Ways to Learn

Ages 3, 4 & 5

600 Great Ideas for Children

Samuel J. Meisels, Ed.D.
Dorothea B. Marsden, M.Ed. ✦ Charlotte Stetson, M.Ed.

GODDARD PRESS
380 MADISON AVENUE
NEW YORK, NY 10017

Book design by Jenkins Group, Inc.

Manufactured in the United States of America.

PUBLISHER'S CATALOGING-IN-PUBLICATION DATA

Meisels, Samuel J.

Winning ways to learn: ages 3, 4 & 5: 600 great ideas for children / Samuel J. Meisels, Dorothea B. Marsden, Charlotte Stetson.

ISBN 0-9666397-6-6

1. Early childhood education—Parent participation—Handbooks, manuals, etc.   2. Education, Preschool—Handbooks, manuals, etc.   I. Marsden, Dorothea.   II. Stetson, Charlotte.   III. Title. IV. Series.

LB1139.35 .P37 M45   2000   00-102856

372/ .21.—dc21   CIP

To the parents and teachers
who have inspired us and
taught us so much.

Acknowledgments

✦

Thanks,

To the A. L. Mailman Family Foundation for supporting this work with a generous grant;

To the University of Michigan for providing the setting that nurtured this work;

To the Joyce Foundation for their assistance in piloting these books;

To the parents who participated in focus groups, read these pages, allowed us to quote them in this book, and offered us the benefit of their wisdom and experience;

To our colleagues Judy Jablon and Margo Dichtelmiller, whose contributions to the Work Sampling System Omnibus Guidelines inspired the organization of the domains and content of these guides;

To Jackie Post for planning, organizing, leading, and summarizing the parent focus groups, and to Ruth Piker, for assisting with the focus groups;

To Mary Brandau, Principal, Kettering Elementary, Willow Run, MI; Kathy Scarnecchia, Principal, Dicken Elementary, Ann Arbor, MI; Lori Fidler, Family Resource Coordinator, Perry Child Development Center, Ypsilanti, MI; and Jane Williams, Director, Willow Run Head Start, Ypsilanti, MI; for facilitating the focus groups;

To Laura Yale and her colleagues at Fairview Elementary School in Milwaukee, WI; Colleen Krajcik, Clarke Street School, Milwaukee, WI; Lesley Straley, Townshend Elementary School, Townshend, VT; Nancy Gerace and Dennis Bell, West Gate Elementary School, West Palm Beach, FL; Nancy Hoff, Gwendolyn Beurnett, and Theresa Torres, Arnn Elementary School, Camp Zama Army Base, Japan; Sam and Ann Morse, Amherst, MA; Eileen Harris, Charlotte County Public Schools, Port Charlotte, FL; Patricia Stevens, Principal, West Early Childhood Center, Midland, TX: Barbara Trube, Principal, Bunche Early Childhood Center, Midland, TX; for reviewing early versions, commenting on them, and obtaining feedback from parents and teachers;

To Patty Humphrey, for her patient, tireless, skillful, and dedicated attention to producing countless versions of these materials, and for coordinating the myriad details that helped bring this project to fruition; and

To Barbara Turvett, whose careful, sensitive, and imaginative editing, and whose knowledge about children and families, touched every page and every idea in these books.

Contents

WINNING WAYS TO LEARN FOR 4-YEAR-OLDS

◆

WINNING WAYS TO LEARN FOR 5-YEAR-OLDS

◆

CHAPTER 1

A Winning Approach for Families and Children

Welcome to **Winning Ways to Learn**. This book is filled with ideas you can use to help your child learn as you go about your everyday activities. You will find that the **Winning Ways to Learn** approach is easy, it's fun, and it works!

This book will help your child become a successful and enthusiastic learner by showing you how to support him* in developing the skills and attributes that are important in the preschool years.

Winning Ways to Learn differs from other teaching aids because its focus goes beyond drill and practice. Research shows us that those children who love to learn and who are also good learners share several important attributes:

They believe in themselves.

They feel competent.

They aren't afraid to take reasonable risks and to fail.

They understand that working toward a goal will eventually pay off.

They are curious and inquisitive about ideas, objects, people, and the world.

The are able to conceptualize and represent ideas.

They find pleasure in the process as well as in the product of their work.

---

* "Him" and "her" are used interchangeably throughout this book. All of the ideas and activities that are described can be used with either boys or girls.

Winning Ways to Learn is intended to help you develop these attributes in your child. Although acquiring factual information is central to learning, it is only one component of a complex and multifaceted process. A child's attitudes are vitally important, too. A simple activity, such as weighing and measuring different household items, not only involves numbers, which must be memorized, but also teaches spatial and conceptual skills.

Activities such as the measuring exercise above can also be turned into games. Find the biggest window! Which box of cereal is heaviest? How many doors do we have? This, too, is important. We know that the learning and emotional centers of the brain are closely related. Having a good time clearly enhances the process of learning. It also makes children want to learn even more. Like the rest of us, children want to do more of what they enjoy.

The activities in this book cover *all* the bases. They will help your child learn a great deal of specific information. But just as important, they will help build a strong foundation for learning in your child. Curiosity, perseverance, higher-order thinking, creativity, imagination, problem-solving—these and many more skills and attributes are all part of the total learning process.

As you will see in this book, you can help your child build this foundation as you introduce her to the possibilities for learning that abound in everyday life. **Winning Ways to Learn** will help you find countless ways to turn ordinary activities into potent learning opportunities.

Using this book as a guide will also help to deepen your respect for your child as a learner. You will gain a better understanding of how your child learns at school and home and how he can become even more successful at it. In addition, the experience and information offered here can increase the pleasure you experience when spending time with your child. You will enjoy being with him during some wonderful moments of discovery. A key to learning for all of us—especially young children—is an openness to change. As parents, **Winning Ways to Learn** can help you become more aware of how much your child is learning and changing.

THE BRIDGE BETWEEN HOME AND SCHOOL

Winning Ways to Learn is more than a learn-at-home primer, valuable as that may be. It will also help build a bridge between school and home, even if schooling takes place at home. This book will help you:

✦ Understand some activities that occur in the classroom.

✦ Notice what your child does at home that reflects what he has learned in school.

✦ Know what to do at home to support and advance your child's learning.

Armed with this information, you can easily create an enjoyable and effective learning environment at home that will consistently support what's being learned and taught in school.

The parent connection is extremely important here. Studies show that when parents are involved with their children's school-related learning efforts, children do better in school. Part of this is the additional time spent on learning. But a big part is a caring parent's personal input, attention, and responsiveness.

You are irreplaceable. Your initiative, encouragement, patience, enthusiasm, and praise cannot be provided by computers or video games. Your involvement will further your child's motivation at school and his learning-to-learn skills in ways nothing else can.

But don't worry. Done properly, this is not burdensome. The **Winning Ways to Learn** activities will become an enjoyable part of daily living, not an extra demand on your schedule.

WHAT'S IN *WINNING WAYS TO LEARN*

This book is divided into three major sections, one for each year, ages three through five. The section for each age covers the following seven major learning areas:

1. Personal and Social Development

2. Language and Literacy

3. Mathematical Thinking

4. Scientific Thinking

5. Social Studies

6. The Arts

7. Physical Development and Health

Each learning area begins with a discussion of what a child of that age should be learning. This is followed by a section labeled *From School to Home*, which tells you how a teacher might help your child learn about a particular area, and how your child might demonstrate this learning at home. The goal is to help you better understand why your child's teacher may use certain activities and how some of your child's naturally occurring questions, ideas, or activities at home are extensions of what he has learned at school.

For example, if you visit your child's preschool or kindergarten classroom you might find the children creating a chart that shows everyone's favorite foods. This activity goes beyond listing the different foods that classmates eat, or guessing the most popular foods. It involves children in the process of discovering the world of probability and statistics, and it does this by helping children learn about aspects of their own world. Through these classroom explorations children discover the meaning of quantity and number, how to apply their growing understanding and skill when making guesses and estimates, and how to keep track of information. They also begin to learn how to read or interpret information displayed on graphs.

At home you might find your child asking you and other family members about your favorite foods, beginning to make charts and graphs about other things (like changes in the weather, who has the most household jobs, and so on), and generally showing more awareness of the world around him. This book will help you understand your child's emerging sense of wonder and control that is so important to his development.

To help make this possible, you will find sections called *It's Your Turn* throughout the book. These sections include over 600 activities and ideas—more than 200 for each age—that you can enjoy with your child. All involve simple materials or experiences that come directly from home, family, and neighborhood. Suggestions include materials to keep on hand, things to do with your child, books to read, and trips to take.

You don't have to buy expensive toys or equipment, and you don't have to know more than you know already as a parent or family member. All you need is a desire to nurture your child's learning and a willingness to engage her in activities that will add to what she can do already.

As you read the suggested activities for each age level, you will see a clear pattern of year-to-year growth on all fronts. You will also find many ways in which a skill in one area supports growth in other areas. For example, conceptual thinking in some of the social studies activities builds skills for math and science, too. In particular, the strengths developed in the personal and social area affect your child's approach to learning in all other areas.

THE SOURCE OF *WINNING WAYS TO LEARN*

Winning Ways to Learn is the product of over twenty years of research, development, and testing. It is a direct descendant of the **Work Sampling System**®, an innovative program used by tens of thousands of teachers nationwide for assessing children's skills, knowledge, behavior, and accomplishments. The **Work Sampling System** was developed to help teachers of 3-year-olds through fifth graders observe, document, and assess children's achievements within the rich and varied contexts of learning. Specifically, it was designed to tell teachers *how well* students are doing by documenting *what* children are doing.

The **Work Sampling System** helps teachers keep track of the many skills and behaviors that are not covered in typical achievement tests. It includes not only the academic subjects of math, science, and reading, but also many subjects, skills, and aptitudes that are central to the learning process, including social skills that are so important to working well with adults and other children.

The activities in **Winning Ways to Learn** are based on those in the **Work Sampling System** that are used to gauge children's performance and that have helped improve children's academic achievement. Like the **Work Sampling System**, the activities in **Winning Ways to Learn** cover the full range of skills that children are expected to develop, and they recognize and appeal to a wide variety of children's and families' interests.

These activities will help you foster your child's special interests and favorite activities. They will also help encourage growth in areas in which your child is only beginning to explore or in which she needs extra help.

BE CREATIVE!

When it comes to your child, you are the expert. That's because, like all concerned parents, you know more about your child than anyone else: what makes her happy or sad, what is difficult for her, and what she enjoys.

The activities in this book can easily be expanded by you and your child. Be creative. Write down new ideas as they come to you, and ask your child and other family members to think of new things to do as well. You will find that some activities will become favorites, and you and your child will go back to them often.

You will soon see how some of the simple, everyday things you do with your child can support her educational growth and can build on what she is learning at school or in other educational settings. These experiences will help your child know more, do more, think more carefully, and use her knowledge and skills more effectively. In short, your child will gain a keener sense of the world and how to succeed in it.

Happy learning!

Winning Ways to Learn
for 3-Year-Olds

CHAPTER 2

Personal and Social Development

✦

The message is clear: When children of any age have confidence in themselves, when they believe in their own ability to try new things, to create, and to explore, they will achieve things—and they will learn. This feeling of self-worth begins to develop early in children's lives, and it can promote their success in the school environment.

Three-year-olds are at a wonderful stage of development. They are eager to please. They love being in small groups where they can practice their social-language skills. Dramatic play takes on great importance as they try out the language of adults and play at family roles, pretending to be a mother, a father, a baby, a doctor, a nurse, or a mail carrier. And they are beginning to relate to other children and to their teachers in a way that will influence their overall school success. For these reasons, both personal and social development represent a vital component of learning. Children's growth in this area can be viewed through their:

Self-concept and self-control

Approach to learning

Interactions with others

SELF-CONCEPT AND SELF-CONTROL

Three-year-olds are eager to please and to understand the roles and rules around them. Yet they often find it hard to do some of the things adults want to teach them, such as sharing or taking turns. Repetition and consistent routines help these preschoolers gain a sense of order in their world. And children thrive on praise and encouragement.

Entering preschool or child care, however, is a big change. Many children need time and support to make the transition and overcome their anxiety. This may mean short visits to the new classroom for the first few sessions. Or it may require a parent staying through the first couple of sessions. A child may need to keep a favorite object—a doll, a truck, a stuffed animal—close at hand for several weeks. With loving attention and ample support, three-year-olds will feel confident about themselves and be able to make changes successfully.

From School to Home

The preschool environment is a wonderful place for your child to grow in confidence and control. Your child may watch and observe other children at play for a while if he is unsure about entering into classroom activities. Eventually, he'll enjoy being a part of his class, playing in small groups, participating in group discussions about books, going on class trips. He'll follow classroom routines: hanging up coats, putting lunch boxes in the refrigerator, washing hands before eating, and cleaning up eating places after lunch. He'll participate in classroom clean-up by learning where to stack the blocks, store the puzzles, and put the books. And your preschooler will respond promptly to some important rules, such as not hitting other people and stopping what he's doing when a bell is rung or the teacher calls his name.

Then he'll bring his new-found sense of self home. Your child will want to duplicate some class routines by, for instance, asking for a special hook so he has his own place to hang his coat. You'll see him put crayons away before taking out a puzzle. He'll insist on washing his hands by himself. He may also invent an imaginary friend to play with and try out newly learned social or language skills. And he'll engage in dramatic play, such as dressing up in Daddy's shoes or Mommy's jacket.

It's Your Turn

To help your child make the most of what he's gained from school:

✦ **Let him do it himself.** Help your child learn to dress on his own.

✦ **Give him some space.** Designate a reachable shelf for your child so he can take out and put away his toys and books.

✦ **Give him a job.** Encourage your child's willingness to assist with chores by letting him help you sort the laundry, pour the soap into the washer, or help you make the beds.

✦ **Have him do what you do.** Give your child his own plastic cooking dishes or simple and safe tools so he can "work" alongside you.

✦ **Co-create routines.** Let him help decide, for example, the order of his bedtime routine: First put away toys, then get undressed, brush teeth, read a story, have a hug, and turn out the lights.

✦ **Follow his lead.** Pretend you are one of your child's school friends and encourage him to choose how the two of you will spend your time.

✦ **Let him feel mature.** Give your child a box of dress-up clothes—a vest and tie, grown-up shoes, a jacket, a special shirt—so he can pretend to be a parent getting ready to go to work.

✦ **Prepare him with books.** Read your child stories that mirror upcoming events in his life, such as a trip to the doctor, the arrival of a new baby, or staying overnight at Grandma's house.

✦ **Practice social language.** As you play with your child, create situations in which he can learn to say hello to a grown-up, say goodbye to friends at the end of a visit, and use words to express feelings or ask for something.

✦ **...and social behavior.** Help him know to ask before touching things at a friend's house or before going into rooms other than the one you are in.

✦ **Ask him to tea.** Play house with your child and invite him to a pretend (or real) "tea" party (he will love to pour you some juice from a small tea pot). By showing him that you enjoy his company, you will help him enjoy and appreciate himself.

✦ **Give him all of you.** Plan a special time each day (even if it is only 10 minutes after a meal or before bedtime) when your child can depend on your undivided attention to talk, read stories, listen to music, build with blocks, or do whatever the two of you enjoy.

APPROACH TO LEARNING

Three-year-olds are usually sunny and agreeable. That's pretty amazing when you consider the many new challenges they face: learning how to behave in new places, being away from family members, and entering school, among others. They are often more afraid of what they imagine might happen than of what really is going on. They may invent an imaginary friend to accompany and comfort them. Although they can be uneasy about trying new things, with encouragement they soon learn to relax and enjoy themselves.

FROM SCHOOL TO HOME

Preschool opens your child to a new and exciting world of possibilities. She has the opportunity to try new activities, such as finger painting or various group games. She marvels at the class pet or the incubating eggs that are about to hatch. She gets to try several ways to put a puzzle together, to build a house with blocks, or to paste things on paper. She knows she can ask adults in the classroom for help in solving problems or trying new activities. And she learns what it means to finish one thing before moving on to the next.

At home your child will try to do things for herself rather than letting you help or even taking your suggestions. She'll be more independent about creating play activities, and you'll see her act out a dramatic play or try out a new art form learned at school. She'll experiment as she designs roads or builds castles in the sand box at the park. Your eager learner will notice new plants and birds or pick up interesting stones on your walks together. She may run to show you a worm or bug she found outside.

"This book encourages me to let my child take risks in her everyday decisions. And her risk-taking can lead to positive consequences, including high self-worth."

IT'S YOUR TURN

To nurture her independent thinking:

+ **Encourage creative construction.** Invite your child to put blocks (pattern blocks, bristle blocks, or table blocks) together in new ways.

+ **Art is everywhere.** Keep a collection of "found materials" handy for pasting, such as bits of ribbon, cut-out shapes, stickers, feathers, leaves, and so on.

+ **Help her express herself.** Give your child markers and plain paper so she can make her own lines and designs. Then have her tell you a story about her drawings, and write down her words to show that you appreciate her creativity.

+ **...and help her help herself.** Guide your child as she figures out how to fit things into a box, clean up a spill, or put on her socks.

+ **Encourage her responsible self.** Involve your child in putting away her toys, hanging up her clothes, and washing herself in the tub.

+ **Have her keep her eyes open.** As you walk or ride in the car together, notice things along the way, ask your child questions, and discuss new and interesting things you observe.

+ **Let the music move her.** Together, listen to a song on tape and either sing, dance, or perform the motions suggested by the words.

+ **Watch TV together.** Enjoy a children's program on public television, and then discuss what happened on the show.

+ **Focus on her comprehension.** Pay attention to whether your child understands what you say or needs you to repeat it.

+ **Read, read, read.** Read favorite as well as new books to your child. Perhaps let her choose a favorite and then you introduce a new book.

+ **Keep up with the times.** Start a weekly calendar with your child that shows which days she will go to school, when Grandma is arriving, the day to go to the dentist, the day the baby sitter will be there.

+ **Listen long.** When your child is trying to tell you or the family about something she did, or about an idea, take time to listen until she finishes.

+ **Play-act together.** Act out pretend stories with your child, letting her be the teacher, or the doctor, or the mother.

INTERACTIONS WITH OTHERS

Although three-year-olds are agreeable and eager to please, they are still learning what it means to be social. The idea of friendship is new; for them a friend is someone you are playing with at the moment. When conflict arises during play, they find a new friend, announcing that the first child is no longer a friend. They need help from adults to learn how to resolve conflicts by saying, for example, "Ask me and don't grab!"

Three-year-olds still play side-by-side—parallel play—but they are beginning to explore playing together—cooperative play—in the housekeeping area or while building with blocks. Also new is their exploration of doing things in unison as they sing and play in groups.

FROM SCHOOL TO HOME

Your child has ample opportunity for social interaction in preschool. He takes part in group games or musical activities. He cooperates in dramatic play with several other children as they pretend that they are a family or that they are going on a trip together. He'll probably try out ways to join in a group activity already in progress. And he works with classmates setting up snacks or cleaning up after eating. He is also learning to ask his teachers for help, to get a turn using a marker without just grabbing for it, or to deal with another child taking the crayons he was using.

Your child will seek more social involvement at home, too. He'll want to be included in family games (although he still may find it difficult to follow the rules). He'll try to arrange taking turns at an activity with a sibling or friend and begin using expressions such as "Let's take turns" or "It's my turn now." And all the reminders from you and his teachers are paying off: He is starting to say *please* and *thank you* in his conversations. He'll also want to say goodnight to everyone in the family before going to bed.

"I like that this section teaches appropriate social cues and responses; it helps my child understand what others are feeling."

IT'S YOUR TURN

Your child will become more and more interactive as you:

+ **Promote those playdates.** Take your child to a friend's house to play or invite one of his pals to your home. A playdate of around an hour is a good amount of time for children this age.

+ **Encourage his creative interaction**—by playing pretend games with your child, talking silly talk, or singing rhyming songs that either you or he initiates.

+ **Teach him to take turns**—by doing just that as you and your child play with a bathtub toy, push a toy train on the tracks, or string beads.

+ **Model manners.** Show your child by example how to greet friends, say hello and goodbye, or acknowledge an introduction; talk with him before and after about what you did.

+ **Have chats.** Engage in conversation with your child while you do things around the house or drive in the car. As you talk together, keep in mind that you want him to learn how to talk to others, be polite, and stay on topic.

+ **Show him you care.** Express your concern when a friend of your child's falls down or when someone is upset. In this way you let him know how to be sympathetic and show it.

+ **Show him how you express yourself.** Let your child know how you feel when you are tired, when you hear a sad story, or when you are happy.

+ **Read about social behavior.** Pick books that deal with being polite, having and being a friend, or going visiting. Some good choices: George and Martha stories by James Marshall or *Sesame Street's Growing Up Books*.

+ **Help him use his words.** Teach your child that words—"I don't like it when you take my crayon. Don't do that"—are better than grabbing or pushing when he is in conflict with a sibling or friend.

+ **Set up social solutions.** Make specific suggestions for settling disagreements: "Your turn is over when the timer rings"; "When *Arthur* is over, it will be your sister's turn."

+ **Change the emotional dynamics.** For instance, when your child doesn't want to leave Grandma's house, let him know you have a special book for him to look at in the car on the ride home.

+ **Television time.** Watch a children's television program such as Mr. Rogers with your child and talk over Mr. Rogers' ideas for ways to be a friend or a helper.

CHAPTER 3

Language and Literacy

✦

One of the most exciting developmental accomplishments of three-year-olds is exploring and becoming skilled at language expression. Children relish the discovery of the power of words and language. As they gain patience for listening to stories, they get better at remembering both stories and past events. They are also beginning to understand the relationship between written language and spoken language.

Children learn to read and write over time in much the same way they learn to talk—naturally and slowly. They become familiar with letters, sounds, and words. They explore books and develop their own ideas and stories. Finally, they learn to sound out and read letters and words and to write them so others can read their ideas. Their progress can be seen in three areas:

Listening and speaking

Literature and reading

Writing

LISTENING AND SPEAKING

Three-year-olds are excited by their newly acquired language skills. The first ones they develop are listening and understanding. In a group setting, such as preschool, children may have a difficult time with these tasks when a teacher is reading or talking to the group rather than to them individually. Teachers help children listen when they give verbal instructions, read to small groups, and set up listening centers where children hear stories on tape while following along in a picture book.

In addition to listening, three-year-olds are becoming proficient in speaking their thoughts. However, they may continue to have trouble pronouncing many words. Some children may even develop a mild stutter as thoughts come tumbling out faster than their tongues can manage. Parents help best by pronouncing words clearly, listening carefully, and being relaxed and patient.

FROM SCHOOL TO HOME

Your preschooler's life at school has a lot to do with language. She listens to short stories during group story time, and she'll wait until her name is called before leaving the circle to get her coat. She listens to classmates as they talk about a trip to the zoo or something their brother did, and she talks to them about things she's done. She may make a request at group time to hear a favorite story or sing a favorite song. And she'll retell a story using puppets or a flannel board.

You'll notice that your three-year-old will listen for longer and longer stretches of time as you read stories to her. Or she'll pay attention as you read her a letter from a relative. She'll use new words learned at school and also ask you for the meaning of a word she heard you use. She'll now join in a family conversation about, for example, planning a vacation.

"The ideas in this section show children the importance of their participation and their interpretation of things."

It's Your Turn

To nurture your child's verbal give-and-take:

✦ **Listen to the world.** Encourage your child to try to identify the sounds you hear as you walk together down the street or in the woods.

✦ **...and to the night.** Listen to the night sounds when you and your child sit outside after dark.

✦ **Train her ear.** Have her listen to stories on tape. This will help her listen to details and work to understand what she hears.

✦ **Do book recaps.** Talk with your child about stories you have read together. Ask her who the characters are, what happened to them, and what her favorite part of the story was.

✦ **Play a listening game.** Try word games, such as you describing the characteristics of an object in the room and your child trying to guess what you are describing.

✦ **Reiterate rhymes.** Read nursery rhymes together, and then repeat them with your child at different times during the day—as she gets dressed, while you are waiting in the grocery store check-out line, when in the car.

✦ **Put her on the phone.** Let your child talk on the phone with a grandparent or relative to give her experience listening to as well as answering questions.

✦ **Play at small talk.** Invent pretend conversations that your child might have at the ice-cream store or when visiting a friend.

✦ **Have her think ahead.** While reading a familiar story, stop and ask your child to tell you what is going to happen next.

✦ **Let her speak for herself.** Encourage your child to give her own answers when people ask you about her in her presence.

✦ **Involve her in family chats.** Include your child in family dinner-table conversations.

✦ **Pretend chat.** Pretend to have a conversation—or reenact a table conversation—helping your child practice her answers or express her ideas.

LITERATURE AND READING

A lifelong love of literature starts in the first years of a child's life. It is important to let children know that there is pleasure in books and the reading of them. Three-year-olds love simple stories, books with lots of pictures, and repetition. They like to browse through a book after the story has been read. You may hear them quietly retelling familiar stories, using pictures as clues. And often the pictures will inspire them to make up their own stories. Through being read to, young children gain listening skills, new vocabulary, and an understanding that the spoken word can be written down.

FROM SCHOOL TO HOME

In preschool, story time is a regular feature. Your three-year-old is growing able to listen to stories read aloud for increasingly longer periods of time. In addition, he listens to stories on tape in the listening center. He may look at picture books during free-choice time, retell or make up a new story using flannel-board cut-outs, and play an animal or a character as he acts out a story with classmates. He might also "read" a rebus-style story, in which pictures are shown in place of some of the words.

At home your little book-lover will ask for favorite stories to be read over and over again. He'll answer simple questions about the stories and talk with you in more detail about the illustrations. He may sit down with a favorite book and "read" it by using the illustrations as memory cues. As you read a magazine, your child may pick up his own magazine and thumb through it in much the same way he sees you looking through your magazine. And don't be surprised if he retells a story heard at school at the dinner table.

IT'S YOUR TURN

Study after study reveals that reading with your child is essential for building knowledge that leads to reading success. To foster your child's love of reading:

✦ **Talk about the tale.** Discuss the characters in the story you just read and recall what they did.

✦ **Tell tales together.** Make up new stories together about characters from familiar books.

✦ **Read about his life.** Choose books that reflect your child's own experiences, such as going to the zoo, playing in the sandbox, and enjoying preschool.

✦ **Go to the library.** Start making regular trips, and encourage your child to help pick out storybooks to borrow.

✦ **Tune in to a tape.** Listen with your child to a children's book on tape (libraries have them), and turn the pages in the accompanying book as the story unfolds.

✦ **Read children's poetry.** Try Mother Goose and Winnie the Pooh rhymes, or poems by Robert Louis Stevenson; repeat favorite selections until your child can recite them with you.

✦ **Read the paper together.** Involve your child in the food section of your local newspaper. Three-year-olds love to hear about and look at pictures of food.

✦ **Create a story board.** Make a flannel board at home; cut out figures to represent characters in stories or original characters that your child can use to tell his own stories.

✦ **Play with your fingers**. Make up some finger plays that you and your child can recite together as you wait at the grocery store, at a traffic light, or in the doctor's office.

✦ **Make books.** Create your own short storybook: Fold a few pieces of construction paper in half and sew them together with yarn; cut interesting pictures out of magazines, paste them in your book, and together create a story to go with the pictures.

✦ **Read, read, and read some more,** to your child, of course!

✦ **...and create a reading routine.** Plan a regular time each day to read to your child, perhaps right after a meal for a quiet time, or at bedtime as part of the "going to bed" routine.

WRITING

Even writing the letters in their name is not common for most three-year-olds. They are just beginning to realize that written symbols can be used to represent the sounds they make when talking. Their attempts at getting thoughts down on paper usually take the form of scribbles, which begin to appear in straight lines and then as jottings across a page. They may tell their parents or teacher what they have written down. Adults can help by listening carefully and writing down children's messages using "grown-up letters."

FROM SCHOOL TO HOME

In school your preschooler dictates her thoughts and stories so they can be written down and read at a future time. She is learning to recognize her name when it is written on papers and other creations. She'll practice making the symbol given to her for identification purposes, and she'll make a mark on the edge of her painting to signify her name. If she indicates interest, your three-year-old may begin to form the first letter (or more) of her name.

Your child will work towards pre-writing as she brings you a page of scribbles and tells you it is a letter to Grandpa; then she'll ask for an envelope to "address" and mail the letter in. She may scribble a list and tell you it's for shopping at the market. She'll watch as you write and then ask you to read what you have written. She'll also ask you to write the letters in her name, or want to "write" a letter using your computer keyboard.

IT'S YOUR TURN

You'll prepare your child for writing when you:

+ **Take dictation.** Ask your child what is in a letter she has "written," then write down what she tells you.

+ **Take more dictation.** After your child scribbles her own shopping list (while you write yours), ask her to read it to you so you can write her words in conventional printing.

+ **Make some room.** Create a space for "writing" for your child where she can find her own pencil and paper and perhaps some stickers for decoration.

+ **Write thank-you notes together.** Have your child draw pictures of her thoughts as you write down her words.

+ **Have her sign off.** Let your child make her personal squiggle to stand for her name on a birthday card you are sending out.

+ **Write captions.** At the bottom of a drawing or collage she's created, write down your child's comments about the piece of art.

+ **Spell it out.** Place some magnetic letters on the refrigerator door and arrange some of them into your child's name; at other times spell out *Mom*, *Dad*, or the name of a sibling. Just have some fun with this rather than turning it into a lesson.

+ **Play the name game.** Make duplicate sets of game cards with letters from your child's name (first and last), your name, and siblings' names; play a matching game with them.

+ **Give her the tools.** Provide lots of unlined paper and pencils or crayons for your child to explore making lines and shapes on paper.

+ **Play "let's recall" together.** With your child, select photographs of her growing up, or of a vacation trip and paste them in her own book. Write down her words about each photo and then look at the album periodically, reading the words to her that she dictated.

+ **Chalk it up.** Hang a chalk board in your kitchen or near your desk where your child can draw shapes and erase and draw again.

+ **Stop!** Point out common environmental signs such as stop signs or McDonald's. Comment about the shapes of the letters such as, "That S looks like a wiggly snake," or "That M is just like your name—they both start with an M."

CHAPTER 4

Mathematical Thinking

✦

Three-year-olds may know some numbers, but they often just learn the sequence of counting without actually understanding about the quantity of a group of objects. They usually cannot count many objects with accuracy as they point to them; if they are able to say numbers in order as high as 5, or maybe 8, they are doing well.

There is much more to mathematical thinking, however, than just counting. There are many concepts children need to grasp. In order to see patterns and the relationship of one thing to another, they need to learn the names of colors and shapes, to understand the idea of size (large and small, long and short), and the meaning of positional words, such as *under*, *over*, and *beside*. Mathematics for young children breaks down into three categories:

Patterns and relationships

Numbers and their use

Geometry, spatial relations, and measurement

PATTERNS AND RELATIONSHIPS

Three-year-olds are just beginning to recognize and use words associated with shape and size. Many children this age recognize and can label colors, but many others still do not understand this attribute. Learning the names of shapes is a great accomplishment. Grouping and categorizing is often beyond three-year-olds' comprehension.

FROM SCHOOL TO HOME

In preschool, your child is beginning to enter a world of simple mathematics. He may separate buttons or other objects into two piles: one pile of big buttons and the other of little buttons. He may also separate his class into two groups: girls and boys. He'll begin to recognize that some classmates are taller and some are shorter. And he'll notice which children are wearing red socks (or shirts) on a particular day and which children are wearing blue socks (or shirts). He may also line some colored blocks or beads into color rows: one row of all red and the other of all blue.

He'll sort and compare at home, too. He may try to figure out whether there are more boys in the family or more girls and then try to decide who is a boy: "Is Daddy a boy, too?" Then he'll look around the table to see if everyone in the family has the same color eyes. You'll see him line up objects—stuffed animals, for example—in a row from biggest to smallest. He may also compare the size of shoes: Who has the longest and who has the shortest? Or he'll draw a set of lines with each line shorter than the one before it.

"These guidelines are very informative; they help to build communication with not only the parent and child but also with the parent and school."

IT'S YOUR TURN

To help your child see differences in color, pattern, and size:

+ **Help him get color-coordinated.** Talk about colors of clothing as you help your child get dressed: "Pick out a pair of socks that will match the green in your shirt."

+ **Tell a story with shapes and colors.** Play with a felt board together: Cut out shapes, figures, and animals in different colors, and name them as you move them around on the board. For example: "Let's find Brown Bear and Pink Pig and have them go looking for yellow honey together."

+ **Make a match game.** Make up matching-game cards with colors or shapes; then you say the color or shape name as your child matches two cards.

+ **...and play established card games.** Teach your child simple games that require matching, such as "Old Maid" or "Concentration."

+ **Plan patterns.** With beads, peg boards, or colored blocks, make or build simple patterns (such as red, blue, red, blue; or yellow square, green circle, yellow square, green circle), always naming the colors and the shapes as you and your child use them.

+ **...and "sound" patterns.** Clap a pattern (2 quick, 1 slow; 1 hand clap, 2 lap claps; or 1 loud clap and 2 soft claps) and help your child clap your pattern along with you.

+ **Create a collection.** Help your child collect acorns, seashells, leaves, or bottle caps, and then organize them according to different rules—size, texture (smooth, rough), or color.

+ **Figure out the neighborhood.** Notice together which trees are big and which are small, which houses are white and which are brown, and how many different colors of flowers there are.

+ **See how signs shape up.** Notice and discuss the patterns and shapes of street signs: "How can you tell that's a stop sign?"; "How can you tell that sign says *Slow*?"; "Look for a sign that tells you a school is nearby."

+ **Library visits.** There are many children's books that concentrate on naming colors and identifying shapes. Have fun reading these with your child.

+ **...and more library visits.** Many libraries also have a collection of puzzles for lending. At age three your child will learn about matching and shapes as he picks up and inserts the correct shape (a car in the car space, a triangle in that space, and so on) into its appropriate cut-out space, getting more and more adept with practice.

+ **Look sharp.** Start looking for patterns on his shirt, on the backs of playing cards, on the birthday paper plates.

NUMBERS AND THEIR USE

Most three-year-olds are beginning to be interested in numbers and amounts. They memorize the sequence of the first three to five numbers and may say them over and over, just for fun. They begin to ask questions like, "How many cookies can I have?" They might recite numbers to their stuffed toys or dolls, and they like number rhymes, such as *One, Two, Buckle My Shoe.* They enjoy simple number picture books, and they use words like "lots" and "more." Nearly all three-year-olds can proudly tell you that they have two eyes, two hands, one mouth, one nose, and so on. And they love to show you how old they are by holding up three fingers.

FROM SCHOOL TO HOME

Your child is beginning to feel a sense of ease with numbers in preschool. With her teacher and classmates she counts the number of children in class every day and sings new songs that involve counting. While she works with manipulatives (for example, shape blocks, beads, or cubes that can be attached to one another) she may count the objects she is using or may notice that the child next to her has more than she does. She listens to and responds to stories that involve numbers and quantity. And she may use number and quantity words when she talks with friends: "I have four beads. Do you have four blocks?" "There are millions of blocks in Jimmy's building."

Expect your child to focus on numbers at home, too. She'll bring home a counting song and feel proud to hold up the correct number of fingers along with the words in the song. She may count the stairs in the house or the squares in the sidewalk while walking along. And watch as she "counts" the number of ants crawling up a tree, not being accurate but having fun saying the numbers. She'll probably ask you which is more, 2 carrots or 3 carrots. And she'll guess the age of a relative, using any number that is within her vocabulary.

"The fact that as a parent I can communicate with and teach my child in any situation, such as while shopping at the market, is a great thing to realize."

IT'S YOUR TURN

You can count on your child to count when you:

✦ **Dress by numbers.** Count out loud as you put on "1 sock, 2 socks"; "1 shirt"; "1 shoe, 2 shoes."

✦ **...and shop by numbers.** Count out loud the number of oranges or cans of soup you put into the basket at the market.

✦ **...and walk by numbers.** Count the steps as you go up or down the stairs, the number of steps from the kitchen to the dining table, the number of houses you pass on your walk around the block.

✦ **...and eat by numbers.** Count out the number of potatoes you'll peel for dinner, or the number of apples you'll slice for a snack, and the number of cookies you're putting on the plate.

✦ **Play and count.** As you pile up blocks together to make a tall building, or line them up for a long train, count the blocks as you add them on.

✦ **Counting mail.** As you look through the mail each day, count out the letters for Daddy, the letters for Mommy, and the number of catalogues that are sent every day.

✦ **Count at the table.** Help your child count out napkins, cups, and spoons so everyone will have one of each at dinner.

✦ **1, 2, 3, 4, sing, sing, sing some more!** Learn school songs that include numbers and then sing them with your child, such as the "One Little Indian" finger song.

✦ **Count by the book.** Read books to your child that include number counting. Without trying to teach her how to count, simply let her hear you counting and then count along with you if she wants. In this way you introduce math ideas as fun and natural.

✦ **Keep counting.** Count the number of bears or flowers on your child's shirt or the number of buttons on the front; find counting opportunities wherever you can.

✦ **Make counting a game.** Create a Lotto board that has numbers to match, and say the numbers for your child when she matches them.

✦ **Arrange some numbers.** Put some magnetic numbers on your refrigerator and play with them together, sometimes arranging them into the number of your house, your phone number, or how many fingers she has. Talk about the numbers as you arrange them.

GEOMETRY, SPATIAL RELATIONS, AND MEASUREMENT

One of the first shapes that young children will respond to and recognize is a circle. Three-year-olds are able to draw circles, sometimes going around and around before they stop. They are familiar with a number of common position words, such as *above*, *under*, and *beside*. And measurement words describing length, size, and weight are a part of their everyday language. The more the adults in preschoolers' lives make conscious reference to these words, the better these children will begin to understand measurement.

FROM SCHOOL TO HOME

In his preschool classroom, your child recognizes and begins to look for shapes while playing with pattern blocks. He identifies several shapes when cutting play dough with shape cutters or pasting a variety of shapes on collage paper. He may act out position words in a song or finger play. He uses measurement words, such as *tall*, *tall*er, *short*, *shorter*, *long*, *fat*, and *thin*. Your three-year-old also measures ingredients for making play dough and may use yarn to measure classmates' heights and then compare the lengths of the yarn.

Give him some paper and crayons and watch your child draw many circles. He may also draw shoe prints on paper and "measure" to find the shortest and the longest. He'll arrange nesting blocks in order from largest to smallest. When you say the book is *under* the magazine *on* the table, he'll know where to look. And he'll show you the way he can jump *over* his toy-train tracks or tell you he is putting his chair right *beside* your chair.

IT'S YOUR TURN

Watch things shape up for your child as you:

✦ **Shape play dough.** Have your child use shaped cookie cutters and name the shapes as he experiments with his play dough.

✦ **Shape and bake.** Let him use shape cutters with cookie dough; name the shapes as he forms them; bake the cookies; and repeat the shape names together as you eat them.

✦ **Watch pictures take shape.** Give your child felt cut-outs in a variety of shapes, colors, and sizes, and play games in which you ask him to put the circle under the stars, put one square above the star, and so on.

✦ **Let his reading take shape.** Borrow story books about shapes from the library.

✦ **Create a shaped collage.** Let your child paste shapes you cut out of various colored construction paper on a collage.

✦ **Seek circles.** Find all the circular-shaped things you can in your living room, while driving to the store, and so on.

✦ **Play up prepositions.** Use position words in a conscious way, such as suggesting that your child put his boots *under* the bench *beside* the stairs.

✦ **Tell him where to go.** Set up an obstacle course, and direct your child to crawl *under* the table, *over* the foot stool, *beside* the chest, and so on.

✦ **Play "Simon Says"**–using a variety of position words.

✦ **Get him to measure up.** Make play dough with your child, letting him measure the cup of flour, the half cup of salt, and the quarter cup of water. (Then have him mix it with his hands!)

✦ **Measure up—II.** Let your child help you measure household things, such as the amount of bubble liquid for the bathtub, the amount of powdered mix for the pitcher of lemonade, or the amount of soap powder for the washing machine.

✦ **Line up a collection.** Together, collect leaves, stones, buttons, and bottle caps, and arrange them from the largest to the smallest or longest to shortest.

CHAPTER 5

Scientific Thinking

✦

When children learn science, they learn a lot more than just facts. They learn special ways of thinking about and discovering their world. They learn that scientists observe things very carefully, ask questions about things they don't know, and investigate to find new information and answers to their questions. This is no less true of the first simple observations and questions of preschoolers than of the complex observations and questions of career scientists.

Science for three-year-olds is mostly looking, wondering, and being excited about every aspect of the world around them. For them practicing science means:

Observing and describing

Questioning and investigating

OBSERVING AND DESCRIBING

Three-year-olds are highly curious and love to watch the tiniest ant crawling across the sidewalk as well as the tallest giraffe at the zoo. They will stop to pick up a twig on a walk in the woods and inspect every detail of it. While it's not always easy to tell how much they absorb from these observations and inspections, this is clearly the beginning of scientific thinking and of becoming an observer. Parents and teachers both need to remember to encourage the natural gift of curiosity that three-year-olds possess.

FROM SCHOOL TO HOME

In preschool your budding scientist makes verbal observations about items on the classroom discovery table. She'll become excited about the details of a leaf she looks at through a magnifying glass. She'll also point out and describe some interesting observations about the classroom pet. Your child is also "observing" with her ears. She will listen to sounds on an audio tape and may try to guess where they come from. In addition, she'll try to identify sounds she hears coming from outside the classroom.

Suddenly she won't just blow bubbles, she'll also comment on their shapes and colors. She may want you to look at the ant or worm crawling on the ground and she may try to describe what she is seeing. Your child may also examine a seashell or leaf collection more closely and begin to notice how some are the same and some others are different. She may notice how adding drops of food coloring to cake batter changes the color of the whole cake. She'll enjoy the feeling of sand between her toes and marvel at the way her feet become buried when a wave washes in and out.

IT's YOUR TURN

To nurture your child's budding curiosity:

+ **Get a make on what you bake.** Turn on the oven light and together watch cupcakes or cookies rise, change shape, and become firm.

+ **...and look at what you cook.** Show your child the way the pancake batter turns from runny to bubbly to firm and brown.

+ **Replace air with water.** Show your child how to fill and then empty a turkey baster or an eye dropper while in the bathtub or with a bowl of soapy water at the sink.

+ **Play with bubbles.** Make soap bubbles in a bowl with a hand beater, add food coloring, and discuss what happens.

+ **Study sprouts.** Plant some seeds in paper cups, let your child water them daily, and watch them sprout and grow.

+ **Observe outdoor growth.** Watch changes in trees, grass, plants, and the sprouting of bulbs as the seasons change.

+ **Marvel at nature's gems.** Collect objects on your walks together—fall leaves, pine cones, acorns, pebbles and stones, seashells, wild violets or daisies—and describe them.

+ **Look up.** Gaze at clouds, the stars, trees, and leaves together, enjoying their various shapes and colors.

+ **Birding.** Together watch the birds that eat at your feeder and help your child describe them. This helps identify colors and size and is part of becoming an observer.

+ **...and classifying.** Begin to look at the different kinds of dogs (or cats, or cows, or fish, or horses; pick an animal group you like), and describe how each is unique. This will be general at first but it encourages noticing details.

+ **Figure it out before you finger it.** Collect pieces of fabric with a variety of textures; guess what each will feel like before touching it, and then touch it to see how it really feels.

QUESTIONING AND INVESTIGATING

For three-year-olds, wondering and speculating about things often comes after spending lots of time just watching. They may quickly forget answers to their "wonderings," but they will be encouraged to continue questioning when adults listen and respond to them.

FROM SCHOOL TO HOME

Your three-year-old's teacher thoughtfully guides children's interests. That's why your child will ask questions about the classroom pet: "Why does it sleep all day?"; "Why didn't it eat the apple pieces I gave it?" He'll wonder about rain or snow: "How did it get up in the sky?"; "Why does it fall out of the sky?" He may watch a bulb grow and wonder if it will ever have a flower. And when he takes a flashlight apart, he'll ask how the batteries make a light. Your child might notice that some things sink and some things float in the water table. He will want to use things from around the classroom to investigate sinking and floating.

Your wonderful child will then wonder at home: where the water goes in the tub when you open the drain; what makes the bubbles in the fish tank; if the stars are lights in the sky that someone is turning on and off; how the firefly makes its light go on and off; what is making that loud noise outside.

"This shows me that science is not just facts. It's about looking at things and how you, your child, and others see things differently."

It's Your Turn

Watch your child marvel as you:

+ **Wonder together**—about things your child finds interesting.

+ **Wonder, yourself.** Comment on all the wonderful and exciting things that surround you every day. Begin to pose questions and then ask, "How could we find out?"

+ **Give him the facts of life.** Answer his "wondering" questions with simple, concrete information, telling your child about things he can or will soon see and hear.

+ **Get him to guess.** Together, think about what would happen to a seed you plant if you don't water it; then investigate planting seeds in two different cups and watering only one cup.

+ **Encourage him to think ahead.** Ask questions, such as, "What do you think will happen to the snow if we take a cup of it inside?" Then experiment by bringing some inside and watching what happens to it.

+ **Think ahead some more.** Guess ahead of time what you might see on your walk in the park or to the store, and then keep track of whether your guesses were right.

+ **Ask your ears.** Play recordings with a variety of sounds on them and guess together what might be making each sound.

+ **Magnify it.** Look at objects such as leaves, a stone, or your skin, through a magnifying glass and describe what you see. Wonder aloud how other things would look if magnified, and investigate.

+ **Wonder about colors.** Using water colors, or markers, or food coloring, find out with your child what would happen if you mixed two colors.

+ **Smell the roses!** Wonder about the various smells and odors as you go through a day. Try to investigate where the smells come from. Try smelling a variety of spices from your pantry, or several different brands of soap. Investigate the smell of cookies or other foods baking.

CHAPTER 6

Social Studies

Three-year-olds are rapidly learning to live with other people and realizing the need to accept others just as they are. They are also beginning to understand how people affect the places they live in. Many lifelong attitudes are established at this early age. Social studies offer preschoolers a growing awareness of these two areas:

People and how they live together

How the past, the land, and people affect each other

PEOPLE AND HOW THEY LIVE TOGETHER

Preschoolers increasingly focus on differences, especially in people who look or act differently from the people they know well. They are also beginning to understand, by talking and exploring, the many ways in which people help one another live in the world. Much dramatic play centers around community helpers, such as fire fighters, police officers, doctors, and store clerks. In addition, three-year-olds are in the early stages of understanding rules and expectations about behavior. They need adults who are supportive and consistent to help them develop inner controls for following rules and behaving safely. Getting to know people who are different from them, visiting and acting out a variety of community roles, and learning to follow a few rules consistently all further three-year-olds' awareness of how people live cooperatively.

FROM SCHOOL TO HOME

Many preschool classrooms offer a diverse community in which children can learn about many kinds of people. Your child will then notice the ways in which children are alike and different: All children have eyes, hair, mouths, and noses, but some eyes are blue and some are brown, some hair is yellow and some is black, some skin is brown and some skin is whiter, some children are taller and others are shorter. A teacher will encourage talk about how families are similar in some ways and unique and special in others. With her classmates your child will act out a variety of family roles in dramatic play: mother, father, baby, big sister. During outdoor play she may pretend to be a fire fighter. And she'll play by the rules of simple circle games, such as "Ring Around the Rosie" or "Wonder Ball."

She'll then come home and tell you about a classmate's family that is different from yours. She may notice and comment on the differences among the people in the store, at the library, or in the park. Your three-year-old wants to play a part in her family's job expectations, so she'll take her plate to the sink after eating. She may ask to stop and watch the road construction crew or the carpenter at work, or she may wonder how the corn gets from the farmer's field to the store. She now notices the way cars follow traffic rules.

It's Your Turn

To increase your child's understanding and appreciation of others:

✦ **Enjoy variety.** Set an example for your child by showing appreciation for the differences in the people you meet or those who live near you.

✦ **Diversify her book list.** Read stories with pictures that include children of various races.

✦ **Encourage inclusion.** Help your child see that it is fun to invite different classmates home to play because each one plays differently; each one has unique abilities, qualities, and interests.

✦ **Taste cultural variety.** Go to ethnic restaurants and talk about the different kinds of food that are served and how the restaurants are decorated.

✦ **Make multicultural music.** Learn a simple song in, say, French or Spanish and sing it with your child, explaining what the words mean in English. There are many children's tapes and CDs available (check the library) that feature international songs in native languages.

✦ **Talk about inside jobs.** Discuss with your child your family's roles and how each of you helps the rest of the family live together.

✦ **Play "restaurant."** To help her appreciate the jobs people do, one of you can be the food server taking orders and the other can be the customer deciding what to eat. Then switch roles.

✦ **Read about workers**—stories about police officers, doctors, nurses, teachers, farmers, and so on.

✦ **Imagine life without...**For example, think with your child about the custodian at school and what would happen if the school didn't have a custodian.

✦ **Encourage her community questions.** Spur her inquiries about how things happen, such as how a cow's milk gets into the carton at the store or how a letter gets from your home to a cousin's house.

✦ **Discuss house rules.** Talk with your child about family rules, such as not hitting. And encourage her to talk about other rules she knows, such as not taking or using other people's things without asking.

✦ **Talk about who's in charge.** Begin to explore ideas about how we need leaders and people "in charge" when people are doing things together, such as having a teacher in a class or a crossing guard at the corner.

HOW THE PAST, THE LAND, AND PEOPLE AFFECT ONE ANOTHER

Even young children can understand that what they do affects the place where they live. If they leave their toys all around, it's hard to walk across the floor and the toys might get broken. If no one washes the dishes after dinner, there will be no clean dishes for the next meal. When adults point out these concepts, they begin to be a part of a child's thinking. Three-year-olds can also see the effects of littering, both inside their homes and in their neighborhood.

FROM SCHOOL TO HOME

Your child has many experiences in preschool that help him see how he and others affect what's around them. He is encouraged to wipe off the table after a finger-painting project so it will be clean for snack time. Or he throws his scraps from a cutting project into the wastebasket. He learns to bring in toys from the school yard so they won't get wet when it rains. He may make up a finger play or a song about not becoming a litterbug. He may also hear in a story how different environments around the world affect the children who live in them.

Don't be surprised when your three-year-old helps pick up the scraps of paper from the floor after wrapping presents for a birthday party; or when he asks the family not to throw papers out of the car window, explaining, "We don't want to be litterbugs." He may wonder why some people throw their cigarettes on the ground, asking, "Won't it start a fire?" or, "Isn't that like being a litterbug?" And he may try to sweep the sidewalk when it is covered with leaves in the fall. He'll point out what's different about someone living in a different climate, for instance, people who live at the North Pole have to wear their winter jackets all the time because it never gets warm where they live.

"These activities help my child see that she can be a positive leader instead of a follower."

IT'S YOUR TURN

You'll help open your child's eyes to the world around him when you:

✦ **Talk trash.** Discuss what it would be like if everyone threw their garbage on the ground instead of taking it to a waste bin.

✦ **Grab the garbage.** Carry a plastic bag with you on your next walk so the two of you can pick up litter.

✦ **Rave about recycling.** Help your child understand the important reasons for recycling as you let him help you separate plastics, cans, and newspapers into appropriate containers.

✦ **Connect to the atmosphere.** Notice the weather and point out to your child that knowing something about the weather helps you decide what to wear.

✦ **Discuss the influence of climate.** Talk with your child about how your environment affects what you can do for fun outside. For example, your cousin who lives in Florida can never go sledding in the snow.

✦ **Read about other places.** Pick books about living in places that are different from where you live. Three-year-olds might like to hear a story about living in Hawaii or Alaska.

✦ **Look at water ways.** Read stories about people who live near a river or ocean and the things they can do because they live near water, such as playing at a beach by the ocean, riding in a boat on the river, or skating on a frozen lake in the winter. Talk about what you would do for fun if you lived in a city or in the country.

✦ **Family history.** Look at photographs of grandparents when they were young and talk about the clothes they wore and what they might have done for fun.

✦ **The neighborhood.** As you walk around your block, notice what neighbors have planted or built in their yards to make them pretty.

✦ **Yard Work.** Talk about where you live and how either an apartment with no yard or a house with a yard affects what you can do for outside play.

CHAPTER 7

The Arts

✦

Three-year-olds love to experiment with all of the graphic arts materials that are available to them in preschool, including paints, markers, crayons, and clay. They also love to dance and imitate the movements of others. The world is an exciting place with lots of opportunities to grow and explore. Most preschoolers want to try everything.

Not only do the arts offer a marvelous outlet for children's creative expression, they present wonderful ways to enhance both large-muscle and small-muscle development. Children this age love to move all parts of their bodies in controlled and planned ways, but they need a lot of practice to become physically skilled. The goal is for children to use as many different kinds of artistic expression as possible. In addition, they are learning to appreciate artistic accomplishments of others. Three-year-olds' progress in the arts can be seen through their:

Artistic expression

Artistic appreciation

ARTISTIC EXPRESSION

Teachers expose three-year-olds to as many forms of artistic expression as they can fit into the preschool schedule. This may include lots of singing, moving to music, dramatic presentations of stories and rhymes, and finger plays. And, of course, there are many opportunities to explore the vast array of graphic arts materials: crayons, finger paints, markers, paper, glue, glitter, clay, and more. The benefits: Children explore materials, create, express themselves, improve their motor skills—and have a great time!

FROM SCHOOL TO HOME

Preschool is nothing if not a center for creative expression. Your three-year-old tries a variety of art and craft techniques: finger painting, painting with water colors, painting at the easel with tempera, scribbling with crayons, drawing with markers, using chalk on varying types of paper, gluing, cutting, and printing. She explores the properties of play dough, experiencing its smoothness, pliability, consistency, and how it can be made into a ball or rolled out flat. Your child also takes part in many creative-movement activities that help develop her coordination and expression, such as dance and circle games. She responds to rhythms played on a tape player or on the piano, and she uses rhythm sticks or claps hands to music or a tempo initiated by the teacher. In addition, she acts out familiar stories with classmates or uses flannel-board figures to tell a story.

You've seen your child's involvement with art for some time. At this stage in her development, she will draw "happy lines" with crayons on paper. She'll sing a "smiling song" learned in school and perhaps show you how to dance like a clown or float like a cloud. She may pretend to be a bunny hopping or a frog jumping. And, if she hasn't done so already, she'll want to dance to music on a tape or the radio.

"This book stresses letting children use their imagination, an important part of early-childhood development that parents need to understand."

IT'S YOUR TURN

To encourage and promote your child's creative instincts:

✦ **Foster her expression.** Keep crayons, colored pencils, and plenty of plain drawing paper handy so your child can draw lines and circles, happy and sad feelings, or a story about, for example, her trip to a farm.

✦ **Let her try textures.** Collect bits of fabric, colored paper, cotton balls, stickers, ribbon, and yarn, and have your child explore the textures and consistencies.

✦ **...and create a collage.** Give your child some paste to mess about with and then paste some of the collected bits (listed above) into a collage.

✦ **Get out the finger paint**–use shaving cream and food coloring to create swirls and lines and dots and dollops.

✦ **Collect the dots.** Let your child explore a paper punch and learn how to punch holes; then have him glue the dots into a design on paper.

✦ **Craft cards.** Together make your own greeting cards with markers, glitter, and pictures cut out of magazines, letting your child dictate messages for you to write inside.

✦ **Inspire art with art.** Put on some music and together draw or paint what and how the music makes you feel.

✦ **Keep singing!** Sing songs you both enjoy as you work around the house or wait for the bus.

✦ **Take time to rhyme.** Read Mother Goose rhymes together and act some of them out.

✦ **...and rhyme on line.** Be ready with some short rhyming poems to recite together when you are waiting in line.

✦ **Play with your fingers.** Learn the finger plays your child does in school and try them out during a quiet time.

✦ **Play with puppets.** Make or buy a few puppets and, as you and your child work them, have the puppets tell stories or hold conversations with each other.

ARTISTIC APPRECIATION

Three-year-olds can begin to appreciate the art of others. They look at drawings in books and paintings on walls. They applaud for the violinist who comes to play for them. They laugh at the clown who performs for them. They also learn to appreciate the work of artists by watching and listening to adults' reactions to creative endeavors.

FROM SCHOOL TO HOME

In three-year-old preschool classrooms, teachers begin to focus children's attention on the artistic expression of others. They will call attention to the illustrations in the book being read and encourage questions about how the artist created certain effects. They will help children become aware of the differences between stories and poems. After watching a short video of an orchestra performance, teachers will lead a discussion about the different instruments that were playing and how they sounded. Parents are invited to visit the class to play their instrument, show their paintings, or help the children with a cooking project.

At home your child might report about the Daddy who came to his school and played his violin. Or he might respond to the music being played on the tape deck or the radio by dancing, jumping, or clapping, and exclaiming about the fun the music helps him have. Your child might begin to look closely at the pictures in the book you are reading to him and notice some specific details in the drawings. And he might become interested not only in the size of the statue downtown, but comment on how hard it must have been to make such a big statue.

IT'S YOUR TURN

To encourage his enthusiasm for works of art:

+ **Focus on the pictures.** Talk with your child about the illustrations in his book, pointing out details and style.

+ **Home in on hues.** Talk about the colors in a painting and how they make the observer feel.

+ **Study the subjects.** Wonder together about the people in drawings—who they might be and what the artist is trying to say about them.

+ **Discuss graphic art.** For example, look at the artwork on a cereal box at breakfast and talk about what the pictures are telling us about the cereal.

+ **Study snapshots.** Look at the family photo album, and talk about the photographs and what they remind you of.

+ **Enjoy a storyteller.** After going to story hour at the library, talk about what the story-teller did to make the story fun to listen to.

+ **Have a chuckle together.** Watch funny characters on a television show and talk about what they did that made you laugh.

+ **Appreciate art everywhere.** Stop and watch street artists as they draw or play an instrument.

CHAPTER 8

Physical Development and Health

✦

Children learn by doing. Since so much of what they do is highly active and physical, it follows that children's physical development and the health of their bodies are very important to their mental development. Three-year-olds will practice a new motor skill over and over. They love to run, gallop, and jump. They enjoy doing new things with their hands. Along with language, body movement is their most compelling area of progress. Children's physical development can be seen in three areas:

Large-muscle development

Small-muscle development

Personal health and safety/self-help skills

LARGE-MUSCLE DEVELOPMENT

Large-motor activity is a three-year-old's focus and joy. Children this age love to try new physical feats, such as climbing stairs using alternating feet, jumping down from the bottom step, riding a tricycle, balancing on a beam, or walking on a line. Each of these activities is a challenge for them, but a challenge that is within their reach.

FROM SCHOOL TO HOME

Your three-year-old is constantly on the move in preschool. She takes part in running, jumping, and galloping games with classmates. She marches to music. She climbs on the jungle gym and up the ladder on a short slide. And she pumps her legs to swing higher and higher.

Take her to the playground or park, and she'll run to the swing set, calling, "I'll get there first." She loves to ride her tricycle around and around, practicing getting on and off, stopping, and turning. Your child will playfully walk on the cracks in the sidewalk. She'll march around the house, waving a makeshift banner or singing a song. Watch her practice jumping from the bottom step of the stairs or kitchen step stool.

It's Your Turn

Boost your child's physical skills when you:

+ **Play catch together**—with a large ball or a bean bag.

+ **Shake an arm or a leg.** Roll or kick a big ball back and forth to each other.

+ **Shoot baskets.** Use a wastebasket or set up a board with a hole in it for your child to use as a target. Then help her aim and throw a soft ball or a bean bag toward and into the hole.

+ **Let her balance on a beam.** Set up a 6-foot-long 2 x 4 board; encourage your child to walk its length; then help her try walking on it sideways, backwards, or on tiptoe.

+ **Hit the playground!** Make regular visits so she can use the climbing equipment and the two of you can enjoy the swings together.

+ **Have nature move her.** If you have outdoor space, start a garden with your child, letting her dig the ground, plant the seeds, and harvest the product.

+ **Cavort in the cold.** If you live in a part of the country where there is snow, go out in the yard with your child and build a snow man, or go sledding together.

+ **Work out to a workout tape.** Encourage your child to do exercises with you in time to the music as you watch an exercise video together.

+ **...and try a kid's video.** Choose a children's exercise videotape, and together do the variety of movements the program suggests.

+ **Make moving fun.** Set up an obstacle course out in the yard or even in the house, where your child climbs over things (chairs, hassock), under things (a table or even the bed) and through things (an open cardboard carton).

+ **Vary the speed.** Walk around the block together taking tiny steps, then long strides, walking really fast and then slowing down to the speed of a turtle.

+ **Follow each other.** Play "Simon Says" and create lots of body motions for her to try. Have her create movements for you to copy.

+ **Shall we dance?** Dance together using silk scarves or crepe paper streamers.

SMALL-MUSCLE DEVELOPMENT

Three-year-olds are just beginning to master small-motor skills with their hands and fingers. Using common tools, such as pencils, crayons, paint brushes, and a spoon, may still be difficult for them. For example, some children this age continue to use a full-fist grasp when holding a crayon or eating with a spoon. However, playing with play dough, water, sand, and other materials allows preschoolers to develop skills as they squeeze, poke, roll, and pour.

FROM SCHOOL TO HOME

In school, three-year-olds' hands are busy hands. Your child plays with a variety of items, such as peg boards, puzzles, table blocks, pattern blocks, Legos, Duplos, beads for stringing, and colored beans or buttons for sorting. He tries many ways to form paper into shapes and sizes, such as folding, tearing, or tracing shapes, and then he pastes the forms onto a fresh sheet of paper. He pours and dumps sand or water into large and small containers, using wrist motions and holding the containers in a variety of grasps. He may use an eye dropper to transfer colored water from one container to another. He also dresses and undresses dolls in the playhouse area.

Your child is likely to be doing a lot with his hands at home, too. He probably scribbles and draws on paper with crayons and markers. And he'll ask to tear his own tape from the tape dispenser. He'll want to roll out dough of his own when you make cookies or biscuits. He'll ask for pouring and filling toys to use in the bathtub. And just as he dresses his dolls or other stuffed toys, he'll insist on zipping or unzipping his own jacket.

"I feel that when the school and the parents are 'on the same page,' it helps kids understand how important their activities are."

IT'S YOUR TURN

To help those busy little fingers:

✦ **Encourage finger fun.** Provide toys that require your child to use his hands, such as Legos, Duplos, puzzles, large stringing beads, or lacing cards.

✦ **Let him draw freely.** Keep unlined drawing paper and crayons available for your child to practice scribbling and create line drawings. While coloring books are fun and fine, be aware that your three-year-old will learn more about using pencils and crayons and his own creativity if he can experiment on blank paper rather than trying to color in pre-drawn pictures.

✦ **Collectively create collages.** Use colored paper, snips of fabric, yarn, stickers, old greeting cards, and magazine cut-outs to craft wonderful designs together.

✦ **Have him play with dough.** Make play dough for your child so he can roll it, twist it, pound it, flatten it with a small rolling pin, and cut out shapes with cookie cutters.

✦ **...and pierce the dough.** Give your child things to stick into the play dough, such as toothpicks, pipe cleaners, straws, cloves, and pegs.

✦ **Get his hands in sand.** Put some sand in a flat cookie tray, and show your child how to make designs with his fingers.

✦ **Play finger games together**—such as "Itsy Bitsy Spider," "Where is Thumbkin?" and "10 Little Indians."

✦ **Give him "hand-y" tasks.** Let your child help with household chores that will strengthen his hand muscles, such as scraping carrots or dusting furniture.

✦ **Let him dress himself.** He can unzip, unbutton, and take off his clothes.

✦ **...and dress his dolls.** Provide doll clothes that have buttons and zippers so your child can try on and take off different outfits.

✦ **Holiday fun.** With your child, paste together paper chains, add stickers and lace to Valentines.

✦ **Feed the birds.** Help your child spread peanut butter on a pine cone to hang outside for the birds.

PERSONAL HEALTH AND SAFETY/SELF-HELP SKILLS

With their newly developing small-muscle abilities, three-year-olds are eager to do as much as they can for themselves. They want to take off their clothes, put on a jacket, brush their hair and teeth, wash their hands, and use a spoon and a fork when eating. And they want to do these things by themselves. It is helpful for their development to give them as much time and support as possible in these endeavors.

FROM SCHOOL TO HOME

Preschool offers three-year-olds plenty of opportunities to develop self-help skills. Your child learns to take care of her own toileting needs—by herself. She washes her hands after toileting and before snack time. She can pour her own juice or water from a small pitcher and throw-away lunch papers after eating. She also puts on her sweater or coat and mittens when getting ready to go out.

At home your increasingly competent child will ask to use a fork as you do when eating a meal and want to pour her own milk at dinner time. She'll pull up her pants after toileting and undress herself when getting ready for bed. She'll brush her own teeth at the appropriate times. And she'll proudly show you the way she's learned to put on her coat or sweater at school.

IT'S YOUR TURN

To help your child help herself:

+ **Be firm, contain germs.** Teach your child to cover her mouth when she coughs, and to discard used tissues in the wastebasket.

+ **Teach her correct bathroom habits**—how to use the toilet, wipe herself properly, flush the toilet, wash her hands really clean, and dry them afterward. Keep reinforcing these important self-help skills.

+ **...and make it easy on her.** Be sure your child's pants are easy to pull down and back up again by herself; give her a step stool so she can reach the tap; hang her hand towel within easy reach.

+ **Bathing can be fun.** Help her learn to wash her own tummy, arms, legs, and toes in the tub.

+ **So can brushing teeth.** Show your child how to brush all her teeth, inside and out, and how to rinse. Brush your teeth at the same time.

+ **Prep her to set a place.** Ask your child to help set the table, showing her on which side of the plate to place the spoon, fork, and knife.

+ **Encourage eating etiquette.** As your child feeds herself at the table, show her how to hold her spoon so that it twists easily and doesn't spill on the way to her mouth and how to hold and use a fork.

+ **Prepare pourables.** Put juice and milk into small pitchers so your child can pour her own drinks. The more she does this, the less she'll spill.

+ **Let her serve herself.** Put food on the table in serving dishes so that your child can help herself, thereby promoting manual coordination.

+ **Wipe up spills.** Show your child how to use a sponge or paper towel to mop up her own spills.

+ **Have her be responsible for her stuff.** Ask your child to help you put her toys away, straighten the books on her shelf, or organize her blocks by matching shapes and sizes.

+ **Let her ease into outerwear.** Allow enough time before going out so that your child can put on her own sweater, coat, hat, and so on.

+ **Talk safety.** Begin to discuss safety rules, such as waiting for an adult before crossing the street, not running across the street, not touching the hot stove or oven, and not pulling on electric cords.

Winning Ways to Learn
for 4-Year-Olds

CHAPTER 9

Personal and Social Development

✦

This is the first year of school for some four-year-olds, while others have been in group care since infancy. Whatever their experience, most children this age are ready to explore their relationships with others in a concrete way. They are able to figure out strategies for playing together cooperatively. They are beginning to under-stand the reasons for rules, both in the classroom and while at play. And they are exploring the meaning of friendship. The way they relate to other children and to their teachers plays an important part in their overall school success. For these rea-sons, both personal and social development represent a vital component of learn-ing. Children's growth in this area is viewed through their:

Self-concept and self-control

Approach to learning

Interactions with others

SELF-CONCEPT AND SELF-CONTROL

Four-year-olds tend to enter groups with either bravado or timidity. They are just beginning to understand who they are outside their families, and this means they have to learn who is in charge and what they can decide for themselves in a new context. They are figuring out how to manage their world and control their behavior. To do this they must experiment, observe, and have opportunities to explore. They need consistency in routines and expectations, and they need help from parents and teachers in developing skills that enable them to be simultaneously independent and cooperative in a group setting.

FROM SCHOOL TO HOME

Preschool provides many opportunities to strengthen your child's control and confidence. She has many opportunities to find, use, and put away materials (puzzles, art materials, books, blocks, and so on) for independent play. She chooses activities and stays with them until they are completed. Your four-year-old is learning to use books in a careful and respectful manner. She washes her hands before snack time and helps set out the snack and clean up after eating it. She also puts on her own coat or sweater or practices buttoning and zipping dress-up clothes during fantasy play.

At home your preschooler will perform the self-help skills she's learning in school—dressing, cleaning up after meals, taking out and putting away play materials. She'll want to help with chores around the house, such as straightening up or emptying wastebaskets. Watch and listen as she shows the family a new "finger play" or "reads" a book brought home from school. She may even become the teacher with playmates or a younger sibling, giving lessons, assigning tasks, or organizing a story to act out. She'll insist on following regular bedtime rituals, such as reading and saying goodnight to family members and toys. Then your big girl will brush her teeth without being reminded and put her clothes in the hamper.

It's Your Turn

To help your child make the most of what she's gained from preschool:

✦ **Give her a job.** Let your child help with household chores—setting or clearing the table, sorting laundry, pouring soap into the washer, putting away clothes in their proper drawers, emptying wastebaskets.

✦ **Create a chart together.** Have your child check off the tasks she has completed each day, such as feeding the family pet each morning or making her bed. Her sense of mastery will grow as she charts and sees clearly all that she has accomplished.

✦ **Let her do for herself.** Allow time for your child to dress herself in the morning, and ask her to help pick out school clothes the night before.

✦ **Let your child make reasonable choices and decisions,** such as which book to read at bedtime, which crackers to buy at the grocery store, or whether to have applesauce or pears for dessert. In this way you encourage her to become an independent thinker.

✦ **Be her scribe.** Write down your child's thoughts and ideas when she tells you about her day, dictates a message she wants to give Dad, or relates a story she has created.

✦ **Follow her lead.** Let your child choose the activity or game you will play together during your one-on-one time together.

✦ **Have her make a timely plan.** Let your child help plan a morning routine that will get things done on time.

✦ **Foster her responsible self.** Encourage your child to put her toys and materials away when she's finished using them.

✦ **Create rituals**—establish routines for going to bed, getting ready to ride in the car, going to school or child care, saying goodbye, and so on. Rituals help young children feel safe and in control.

✦ **Exchange rules.** Show your child how to look both ways or follow the traffic signals before crossing the street, and then make her feel important by letting her tell you when it is safe to cross.

✦ **Read about feelings.** Choose stories that have characters dealing with anger, sadness, or fear. Some good examples are *Where the Wild Things Are* by Maurice Sendak, *Alexander and the Terrible, Horrible, No Good, Very Bad Day* by Judith Viorst, and *Sesame Street's Growing Up Books.*

✦ **Comfort her.** It's fine to let her take a familiar object to bed or have a night light on. Also, take her imaginary fears seriously and talk with her about them.

APPROACH TO LEARNING

Preschoolers are naturally curious about everything and love to ask questions. They are comfortable with familiar things and relish routine. In addition, they are usually interested in new adventures as long as a parent or friend is nearby. Many four-year-olds are great explorers and enjoy building with a variety of toys and materials, pretending as they play and create. With adult support, they enjoy trying out new ideas and taking on new challenges.

From School to Home

The preschool classroom is an environment of wonder for your child. He gets excited as he observes new exhibits on the nature table or, perhaps, as he checks to see if incubating eggs have hatched overnight. He questions why sand won't flow through the holes in a sieve or why a block tower keeps falling over. With blocks, your preschooler may build a runway or hangar or a waiting room, using information from a class visit to an airport or hospital. He makes signs for constructions or structures built with blocks or Legos. And he sculpts with real clay or designs patterns with finger paint. He'll bring books or other information from home about something he's studying in class.

Your child will then come home filled with curiosity about all kinds of things: "What's inside the egg? How does it turn into a chicken?"; "How does the runny batter turn into muffins in the oven?"; "Where does the water go when you empty the tub?"; "What makes the light go on in the refrigerator?" Outside, he'll study earthworms and ants as they crawl around on the ground. He'll want to play out in the rain, splashing in the puddles and mixing up the mud. Your four-year-old may bring you a wildflower from the yard and ask you what it is called. And he'll certainly want to invite a friend home to play a special game or ride in his new wagon.

"I especially like the activities we can do at home that help my child get ready for kindergarten."

It's Your Turn

To nurture your child's growing sense of discovery:

+ **Go to the library.** Help your child find books he'd like to take home.

+ **Spark his problem-solving sense.** Ask your child to think of ways to do things—for example, how to draw a boat or make a bridge with Legos. This will encourage his flow of creative ideas.

+ **Schedule a vacation together.** Make a calendar that shows how many days until a vacation, and illustrate the plans for each day of the vacation with drawings or pictures cut from a magazine.

+ **Let him plan a playdate.** Invite a friend of your child's to visit and then plan together what to have for a snack, what to play, and how to know when it's time for his friend to go home.

+ **Show him the step-by-step scheme.** Help your child see all the steps in an activity, such as choosing a game, inviting people to play, picking the place to play, and cleaning up at the end of the game.

+ **Point out the fine points.** Encourage your child's curiosity by asking questions about things you see on a walk or discussing things you see in the pictures of a book.

+ **Have him finish the tale.** Ask your child to make up his own ending to a story.

+ **Help him express himself.** Give your child materials for a collage, then help him come up with creative ways to show a dream or a special feeling.

+ **...and draw on his experiences.** Give your child colored markers and suggest he create a drawing that tells about a trip to the zoo, a farm, or his grandparents' house.

+ **Let the music move him.** Together, listen to a song on tape and either sing or dance to it, or perform the motions suggested by the words.

+ **Watch TV together.** Enjoy a program on public television, and then talk about the ideas expressed on the show.

INTERACTIONS WITH OTHERS

Four-year-olds possess boundless energy and active imaginations. They are in the process of moving from parallel play, in which they engage in side-by-side and often independent activity, to cooperative play, in which they share ideas or create activities together. As they begin to explore aspects of friendship, they may exclude others or become bossy or protective. They are very interested in pleasing adults and are easily influenced by what they *think* an important adult wants to hear. They express their desires and feelings actively, often physically, and may need adult guidance to learn how to manage their aggressiveness. Pre-kindergartners are friendly and eager, often challenging acceptable limits of behavior.

FROM SCHOOL TO HOME

Your child has ample opportunity for social interaction in preschool. She plays cooperatively with two or three other children, whether during dramatic play, at the sand table, or while working with blocks. Sometimes she will follow a leader and sometimes she will direct the action. She joins others in simple games such as "Wonder Ball," "Follow the Leader," or "Simon Says." Your active four-year-old is creative and imaginative in group dramatic play. She is learning to use words to express anger rather than grabbing or hitting. And she'll ask for help when one child wants a toy that another child is using.

Your sociable child will then come home and ask the family to play some of the games she's learned at school. And she'll probably explain the rules for taking turns when playing a game. She'll ask to have a friend visit for a whole day or stay overnight. To engage in creative fantasy play, she'll want to use things from around the house as props or scenery. When she and a friend are taking turns on her bike, she may ask you to set a timer. And she won't be shy about telling a sibling to *ask* when he wants to look at her book, rather than just grabbing it.

IT'S YOUR TURN

To help your child sharpen social skills:

✦ **Make manners matter.** Encourage your child to say *good morning*, *good night*, *thank you*, and *please*. Explain to her that others appreciate and want to be around someone who practices these behaviors.

✦ **Help her talk to grown-ups.** Introduce your child to your friends or other adults and encourage her to say hello, shake hands, and use their names when greeting them.

✦ **Teach her to share.** When a friend visits her, suggest that your child invite the pal to play with her toys and also explain to her friend the rules of your house.

✦ **Encourage empathy.** Help your child understand others' feelings by talking about how a child who fell down might feel or what a child new to the neighborhood might be going through.

✦ **...and inclusion.** Talk about how it must feel to be in a wheelchair or unable to see, and discuss ways you and your child could help that person become a friend.

✦ **Let her in on conversations.** When your child is present don't talk *about* her, talk *to* her.

✦ **Talk over upsets when they are over.** Help your child think about how she can calm down before she gets angry the next time.

✦ **Read and discuss books about feelings.** Stories that include children who are expressing themselves or settling conflicts with friends will help your child with her own social interactions. Two good examples: *Yoko* by Rosemary Wells and *Stevie* by John Steptoe. Also, ask your child's teacher for more story suggestions.

✦ **Help her use her words.** Teach her that words—"I don't like it when you take my book. Don't do that"—are better than pushing or hitting when she is in conflict with a sibling or friend.

✦ **Model emotionally sound behavior.** Express *your* feelings in words when you become angry, and explain why you are upset.

✦ **Try some TV talk.** Watch the shows your child likes with her, and talk about your feelings about what you have watched. (Limit the amount of TV viewing to one to two hours daily, and select programs you feel have some educational value.) If, by chance, your child sees violence on television, whether in the news or entertainment, talk with her about what she's just witnessed. Help her put it in perspective.

CHAPTER 10

Language and Literacy

✦

Excitement about stories and books is one of the most important attitudes children can develop in their pre-reading years. Some children enter school with this attitude already firmly in place because books and reading have been an integral part of their home life. Other children are not as familiar with books. This pre-kindergarten year will inspire children's enthusiasm for storytelling as well as for recognizing their own thoughts and putting them down on paper.

Children's progress in reading and writing is seen in:

Listening and speaking

Literature and reading

Writing

LISTENING AND SPEAKING

Four-year-olds are just learning how to listen as part of a group. This requires a different kind of concentration than one-on-one conversation with an adult. Understanding what is being said, grasping the ideas in a story, and being able to follow general directions are all skills preschoolers will be sharpening.

Four-year-olds are also learning to speak with clarity and to communicate their thoughts. At this point their pronunciation is generally good enough to be understood easily. They are fascinated with the sound of language and will make up long lists of rhyming words, often including nonsense words. They may tell jokes that they find hilarious but that have little or no meaning to adults.

FROM SCHOOL TO HOME

Words are at work in your four-year-old's classroom. He listens to stories read to the class and then answers questions about them. He may choose to listen to a story on tape and follow along in a book as the story progresses. He uses new words or explores ideas learned from class discussions and stories. Perhaps he'll take part in small group discussions about class rules, class activities, or plans for a class trip. He's now able to follow school routines and schedules, and he understands directions and information given by his teacher.

His growing language skills help your child listen to and participate in family conversations. And he is now able to help plan a family event, such as a trip or celebration. He'll ask you the meaning of new words he hears. He'll more accurately respond to your requests, such as, "Please bring me the newspaper from the kitchen table." Your preschooler may now ask to talk to a grandparent on the phone and then have a meaningful conversation. When you read or tell stories at bedtime, he's now able to sit still for considerable lengths of time.

"Following the strategies in this book for helping my child learn has also helped the two of us grow closer."

It's Your Turn

To nurture your child's verbal give-and-take:

+ **Have family chats.** Talk with your child about important family events, such as the upcoming visit of a relative.

+ **Do the two-step.** Your child is now ready to follow two-part directions: "Please look in the closet for your coat, and put it on before you go out to the car."

+ **Train his ear.** Have him listen to stories on tapes or recordings of action songs. This will help him listen to details and remember what he hears. Perform the actions with him.

+ **Do book recaps.** Recall with your child stories you have read together or heard at the library during story hour.

+ **Let him tell the story.** Have your child explain what he sees in the illustrations of a book that you are reading together.

+ **Have two-way talks.** In conversations with your child about events that you have both attended or stories you have read together, discuss ideas equally rather than just having him answer your questions.

+ **Let him tell the tale.** Have your child help you tell the rest of the family about your trip to the park that morning or who you saw at the grocery store.

+ **Be all ears.** Listen carefully to your child when he is talking to you, or tell him you will give him your full attention when you finish what you are doing at the moment.

+ **Try some television talk—II.** Encourage your child to tell you what he did or did not like about a television program you watched together; share your thoughts about the story and characters to help him form his own ideas.

+ **Build those words.** Encourage your child to ask you about new words he hears. Talk about new words and what they mean. Play a game where you each use the new word in a sentence.

+ **Borrow those tapes.** Borrow book-tapes from the library and help him turn the pages in an accompanying book as the story progresses.

+ **Name, please.** Encourage your child to use people's names when he is talking to them, for example, "Thank you, Mrs. Martin."

LITERATURE AND READING

A major objective in preschool classrooms is having children listen and respond to stories. Teachers can nurture a lifelong love of literature not only by reading to their children, but also by engaging them in all kinds of story activities: They ask children to remember who was in the story; they ask questions that will pique curiosity; they help children feel and understand the events in a story; they provide lots of incentives for choosing to look at books during free-choice time. And this part of their job is pretty easy, because four-year-olds love picture books and they enjoy hearing the same stories read over and over again.

FROM SCHOOL TO HOME

Your child "reads" stories in books using the pictures as memory cues. She also chooses to go to the listening corner to hear a favorite story on tape. She'll think up new endings to stories, "write" her own stories, or tell stories through paintings or dictation. Or she'll re-create familiar stories in the dramatic-play area or on the playground. In addition, she might recite lists of rhyming words or recall descriptive words used in stories.

As you know, your four-year-old loves to read at home. She'll "read" a book she brought home from school, either from memory or by using the pictures as cues. With impressive imagination, she'll make up stories about a pretend trip to the jungle or outer space. She'll ask you to read more wild and adventurous stories than those that entertained her at age three. As you read, she'll now point out small details in the book's pictures, or she'll ask you to find details that she discovered when she heard the book read at school. She may also ask you to tell a story about when you were little. As in school, she'll enjoy creating lists of rhyming—and sometimes nonsensical—words that she rattles off with great enthusiasm.

"Now I know not just to read the story but also to talk to my child about what we read: 'Who's the character? Why did he do what he did?'"

IT'S YOUR TURN

Study after study reveals that reading with your child is essential for building knowledge that leads to learning success. To foster your child's love of reading:

✦ **Create a reading routine.** Set a special time to read to your child every day, such as right after dinner, or when she is settled in bed for the night. Of course, read at other times too.

✦ **Go to the library.** Let her select the subject or theme of stories to borrow and read at home.

✦ **Make joint predictions.** Guess with your child what will happen next in a new story you are reading to her.

✦ **Talk about the tale.** Discuss who was in the story you just read and recall what the characters did.

✦ **Let every picture tell a story.** Cut out interesting pictures from magazines and together make up stories that go with them. Write the stories down as you create them so your child can see the connection between ideas and print.

✦ **Tune in to a tape.** Listen with your child to a children's book on tape (libraries have them), and turn the pages in the accompanying book as the story unfolds.

✦ **Be photo-journalists.** While looking at photos of your child's life so far, tell special stories about her as a baby and as a very little girl. Then let the pictures inspire the two of you to create a book about them.

✦ **Flannel-board magic.** Make a board with a flannel covering. Cut out figures to match the characters in a story or nursery rhyme and act out the story or poem on the flannel board.

✦ **Create a block library.** Organize with a few neighboring families to let your children borrow and lend books back and forth. Have the children tell one another about the stories in their own libraries to help the others know which ones to pick; encourage them to make the stories sound exciting and interesting.

✦ **Don't forget rhymes.** Continue to read and say nursery rhymes with your child. Begin to include poetry by such authors as Robert Louis Stevenson or A. A. Milne.

✦ **Read, read, and read some more,** to your child, of course!

WRITING

Four-year-olds are just beginning to make connections between print and thoughts. They watch as adults write letters, make lists, and record events. They want to write their own stories, so they begin with scribbles. These scribbles turn into letter-like symbols, and eventually into actual letters.

At this age the shape of the letter is the important thing. Their first words (usually their name will be among them) will probably have the letters out of order and in varying places on the page. Eventually, they will put letters and words in left-to-right order, but they may still reverse the letters. They won't understand the importance of positioning the letters until they become much more familiar with the actual process of reading.

FROM SCHOOL TO HOME

In school your child writes his name (a symbol, the first letter, or the whole name) on drawings, paintings, a science project, and more. He may make signs for block buildings or Lego constructions, give messages to classmates, or write a doctor's note after examining a doll. He also copies words to make an invitation or a card for a friend. In addition, he expresses his thoughts and ideas by drawing pictures, for example, of his favorite toys, his family, favorite animals, foods he likes, and things that make him happy. He may draw something he imagines, such as what he thinks he'll see during a class visit to a farm.

Your child will continue his pre-writing efforts at home as he puts his name on a dictated letter to a relative or a friend. He may draw the symbol that is used at school to designate his cubby or cup. Enjoy his efforts as he shows you a page of scribbles and tells you the story the scribbles are meant to represent. He'll most likely ask you to show him how to write his name and, later, how to write the names of family members. He may also ask you to write out the stories he dictates to accompany the pictures he draws.

IT'S YOUR TURN

Your child will learn more about writing when you:

✦ **Create a writing center.** Set up a space for your child near where you spend a lot of time in the house. Keep it stocked with paper, pencils, markers, Scotch tape, stickers, and so on. Every once in a while add a surprise such as a new marker or interesting paper for him to discover and use.

✦ **Sign his name.** To help your child recognize his name, write it on a sign that you attach to his bedroom door.

✦ **Focus on the shapes.** Help your child see the shapes of the individual letters in his name as you draw them.

✦ **Then have him sign his name.** Let your child write his own name on letters you send to relatives or friends.

✦ **Make chalk talk.** On a small chalk board (or Magna Doodle or Etch-a-Sketch, if you have one), encourage your child to try writing letters and pictures that he can erase and do over as many times as he wishes.

✦ **Use sign language.** Encourage your child to try drawing signs you see on your walks or trips, such as a stop sign or the McDonald's arches.

✦ **Let him make a list.** Have paper and pencil ready so your child can make his own shopping list for your trip to the store.

✦ **Take dictation.** Encourage your child to tell you his ideas, and then write them down for him. Or have him put the ideas on paper in the form of pictures, which you can then label for him to send to relatives.

✦ **Take more dictation.** After a trip or vacation, encourage your child to draw pictures and dictate stories about it as you write down his words for him.

✦ **Make a story album.** Paste vacation photos in an album or notebook and write down what your child tells you about them.

✦ **Write cards and letters together.** Ask your child to dictate a letter of thanks or an invitation to a relative or a friend.

CHAPTER 11

Mathematical Thinking

✦

Four-year-olds are just beginning to understand what a number really is and what it represents. They are often able to count up to 20 or more by rote. It is more difficult for them to count past 5 or 10 when they are counting actual objects. Once they become more adept at this skill—referred to as counting with one-to-one correspondence—they will still need lots of experience and practice before they understand that counting out 10 crayons means there are actually 10 crayons in the pile. This is the concept of quantity.

When they understand the meaning of numbers and quantity, pre-kindergartners will start to use numbers and counting to solve problems: For example, "How many napkins do we need so that each person at the table will have one?" Growth in mathematical skills for young children is seen in three categories:

Patterns and relationships

Numbers and their use

**Geometry, spatial relations,
and measurement**

PATTERNS AND RELATIONSHIPS

Children need to know several things before they can sort and categorize. They need to be able to label and match colors. They need to know what a shape is and the names of some shapes. They need to know that a pattern involves repetition. They need to understand quantity: tall and short, heavy and light, more and less. They need to see what makes things alike or different from each other. For four-year-olds, thinking mathematically means relating one thing to another, seeing patterns, and understanding how things go together.

FROM SCHOOL TO HOME

In her preschool class, your child has fun sharpening her math skills. She may sort a pile of buttons or a box of crayons by color. Or she may line up a pile of counting rods from shortest to longest. She'll see visual patterns, such as a border around a book cover, or hear sound patterns made by rhythmic hand-clapping or foot-stomping. Then she'll identify and copy a pattern of clapping or a beat on the drum. She may copy or create color patterns when stringing beads or lining up pegs. And as she works with pattern blocks, she'll explore the many ways that they fit together.

Your four-year-old has lots of sorting and pattern-related activity to do at home, too. She may arrange a set of nesting dolls from smallest to largest, or organize her toys into categories: "Stuffed animals go here, blocks over here, and trucks go on this shelf." Notice as she separates her dark-colored dresses from her light-colored ones in her closet. She may express herself artistically by drawing patterns with crayons—two red lines next to two blue lines, for example—and then ask you to guess what should come next. She'll notice the pattern on the rim of your dishes, or point out the repeated pattern on a T-shirt or sweater.

"The fact that as a parent I can communicate with and teach my child in nearly any situation, such as while shopping at the market, is a great thing to realize."

IT'S YOUR TURN

To help your child sort and organize:

✦ **Play the match game.** Make up games in which you and your child match numbers, shapes, or letters. For example, a Lotto board made up of a variety of shapes, shapes in various colors, letters of the alphabet, or numerals. Make a duplicate set of cards and take turns drawing a card to be matched to the pictures on the board.

✦ **Put her books in order.** Help your child arrange her books on a shelf by category: animal books, counting books, books about families, books about feelings, and so on.

✦ **Sort or connect blocks by color.**

✦ **...and then line them up.** Connect blocks into various lengths, and then arrange them from shortest to longest.

✦ **Figure out the market.** Point out how food in the grocery store is organized: cereal in this aisle, canned fruits in this aisle, paper goods over here, and so on.

✦ **Figure out the market—II.** On another trip to the grocery store ask your child to guess in what category items from your list might be found.

✦ **Point out the patterns**—on a cereal box, around the edge of the rug, in a neighbor's garden.

✦ **Set a pattern example.** Arrange buttons, crayons, or game pieces into different patterns and see if your child can continue the patterns.

✦ **...with blocks, too.** Use connecting blocks, such as Legos or Unifix cubes, to create patterns for your child to duplicate.

✦ **...and with a peg board.** Create patterns or sequences with pegs on a peg board and see if your child can continue them. Then remove one of the pegs while your child shuts her eyes and ask her which peg is missing.

✦ **Then turn the pattern tables.** Let your child create patterns that you try to duplicate.

NUMBERS AND THEIR USE

Most four-year-olds can usually count from memory (called rote counting) to 10 or even 20. They can also count as many as five objects as they point to each one. They may or may not yet understand the quantity of five, that is, knowing that when you *count* five cars, you *have* five cars. And they are still figuring out the meaning of more and less, and longer and shorter. They love counting when it's part of a song or a game, but they usually do not like to be quizzed or asked to answer questions about numbers. They begin to feel the power of using numbers to figure things out and solve problems when they can explore and experiment with a variety of materials.

FROM SCHOOL TO HOME

Your four-year-old is sure to do a lot of counting in school, whether he counts along with the class to see how many children are present, counts out napkins and cups for snack time so that everyone will have one, or simply checks how high he can count from memory. He may also count the colors on his classmates' shirts to figure out which color there is more of. And he'll sing counting songs and play counting games.

Expect your child to focus on numbers at home, too. He'll count out the number of cans of apple juice you bought, or he'll ask you to help count cookies to take to school so that everyone will have one for snack. He'll tell you, for example, that there are five people in the family and so you need five glasses on the table. Or he'll wonder how to divide six cookies so that four people will have the same amount. Your child will count the number of houses on your side of the street or the number of doors on your floor in the apartment building or the number of steps from the sidewalk up to the porch. Enjoy numbers with him as he sings a counting song to you or shows you a counting book and counts the objects on a page.

IT'S YOUR TURN

You can help your child to count when you:

✦ **Block out the numbers.** Build block structures together and count how many short blocks it takes to equal one or two long blocks.

✦ **Hit the road counting.** Count together how many stop signs, traffic lights, or gas stations there are between where you live and the supermarket.

✦ **Cook by the numbers.** Decide and count out together how many carrots you will need if everyone in the family is to have one for dinner.

✦ **Play board games** in which you have to count out squares to move ahead.

✦ **Play card games,** such as "Concentration" or "Crazy Eights," and keep track of how many cards each person has.

✦ **Figure it out, out loud.** Count, for example, the daisies your child brought to you as you place them in a glass of water.

✦ **"Guesstimate" the numbers.** Each of you guesses who has the most of something (green beans for dinner, or crayons in a box) and then count the quantities to know for sure.

✦ **"Guesstimate" again.** Guess how many dogs or cats you will see on the way to the grocery store and then keep track of them to see if you were right.

✦ **Read by the numbers.** Find counting books in the library and, as you read them, count the objects in the pictures together.

✦ **Count on life.** As you go about your daily routine, count the number of steps leading upstairs, the number of buttons on his shirt, the number of spoons on the table, and so on.

✦ **Tally your digits.** Count out the number of fingers on each hand, and then count toes; talk about having the same number of fingers and toes on each hand and foot.

✦ **Refrigerator learning.** Keep a set of magnetic numbers on the refrigerator to help your child become familiar with the numerals. Put up the numeral for his age, for your age, for the days until his birthday, or other important events.

GEOMETRY, SPATIAL RELATIONS, AND MEASUREMENT

Many four-year-olds are just beginning to understand the concept of shape as something separate from other qualities of things, such as color or size. Other children can already identify the names of several shapes and can draw some of them. Children this age are busy learning and understanding positional words: *above*, *below*, *beside*, and so on.

They are also interested in comparing things: "Who is older?"; "Which goes faster?"; "Who has more ice cream?" Their concept of measurement is related to their own experience. For example, they will say that something is *more* if it is taller or longer, without noticing the actual amount. Children won't understand the reality of time until they are closer to age eight. Preschoolers relate to time according to concrete experiences: "Riding to Grandma's house is as long as two *Sesame Streets*."; "It will be my birthday after the sun comes up three more times."

FROM SCHOOL TO HOME

In her preschool classroom, your four-year-old works with shape puzzles and shape boards or creates geometric forms with a geoboard, using rubber bands around pegs. She labels a variety of shapes while pasting together a collage. And she tries new positional words—*underneath*, *beside*, *next to*—as she plays games or gives directions for where to find something. She plays group games that use positional words, such as "Simon Says." Your child weighs objects on balance scales, experimenting with what balances something else. She also measures out ingredients for a cooking project using standard measuring cups and spoons.

When she's with you she'll point out shapes on traffic signs or product labels. You'll hear her chant "up, up, up" as she climbs stairs or "down, down, down" as she descends. Your child will use positional words to describe the location of a book or other object: "It's *up* on the *top* shelf *next* to the *big* red book." She'll want to measure family members to see who is shorter and who is taller, and she'll ask you to help weigh each family member on the bathroom scale.

IT'S YOUR TURN

Watch things shape up for your child as you:

✦ **Collect and sort shapes.** Together, cut a variety of shapes from construction paper or old magazines and sort them (by shape, of course) into different boxes.

✦ **Shape up your road trips.** As you ride in the car, see how many shapes you can find on signs, in the architecture of buildings, in clouds, and so on.

✦ **Play "Tic-Tac-Toe,"** using circles and squares for one game, then triangles and crosses for another, and so on.

✦ **Match up shapes.** Play shape-matching games, such as "Lotto."

✦ **Play "I Spy,"** using shape or position words as part of the secret to be discovered. "I see something that is round and is on top of the stove. What is it?" or "I see something square that is on the wall above the table. What is it?"

✦ **Direct your child with positional words.** Give instructions for finding something or putting something away: "Look for it on the *bottom* shelf"; "Put it *beside* your cup"; "Look *under* the book."

✦ **Play positional hide-and-seek.** Have your child ask position-word questions—"Is it *above* my head?"—to discover where an object is hidden. Or you use position words— "It's *near* something that's round"—to lead her to the hidden object.

✦ **Measure by your own standards.** For example, measure the growth of a plant using lengths of yarn. This will help your child grasp the concept of measurement before she uses standard measuring tools.

✦ **Get her to measure up.** Ask your child to measure out the dry ingredients for a recipe using measuring cups and spoons.

✦ **Chart those changes.** Start a growth chart of your child's height and weight, and talk about the changes as you observe them together.

✦ **Track the days.** Create a family calendar and mark off days before a special event, such as a family vacation or a grandparent's visit.

✦ **Talk in terms of time.** Use words such as *yesterday, tomorrow,* and *today* to recall events, to plan ahead, or to talk about activities.

CHAPTER 12

Scientific Thinking

✦

Learning about science continues to teach children much more than facts about the world around them. Scientific inquiry teaches them new ways to ask questions and find answers, as well as new ways to observe and study their environment. For a four-year-old, learning science means:

**Observing, questioning,
and investigating**

Explaining and predicting

OBSERVING, QUESTIONING, AND INVESTIGATING

Four-year-olds, probably above all else, are curious and inquisitive. They often have difficulty staying focused on a task because their great curiosity and the compelling wonders of their world distract them. At age four, children are not ready to absorb abstract concepts or understand things they cannot see. A goal in preschool, then, is to help children see more and begin to talk about what they see. When an adult encourages a child's questions, both adult and child are excited by the process.

FROM SCHOOL TO HOME

In school your young scientist is beginning to use tools, such as a magnifying glass or a microscope, for observation. At the water table, he may examine what happens to bubbles made of colored water when they are blown through a clear plastic tube or straw. He'll test to see what objects are or are not attracted to a magnet. As your child observes ice or snow melting in a dish, he'll talk about quantity ("It seems to get smaller") and temperature ("It's getting warm"). He may watch a tulip bulb grow in the classroom and chart what happens over time. Or he may help care for the classroom guinea pig and notice what it eats.

At home he'll be inspired by his classroom activities to play in a dishpan of bubbles and blow through a straw. He'll also test to see which things (toys, soap, sponge, cup) sink or float in the bathtub. He'll probably want to pick up a caterpillar and put it in a jar to watch what it does. Or he'll observe that the radish seeds have sprouted in your garden and wonder why the cabbage seeds are not yet growing. Your child will notice that the stars in the sky come out one at a time—and then, suddenly, there are millions!

"It is fascinating to see how science helps your child to see things in his own unique way."

IT'S YOUR TURN

To nurture your child's budding curiosity:

✦ **Make tracks.** Observe the tracks your child makes in the sand at the beach. Then observe the tracks of other people and decide which direction they were going in.

✦ **Collect leaves together.** Look at the different kinds of edges and textures; get a book from the library and try to find out which trees the various leaves came from.

✦ **Seek out seeds.** Collect seeds from different fruits—oranges, grapes, watermelon, plums, pumpkins—and encourage your child to use words to describe their differences; cut the seeds open and explore their insides.

✦ **Grow things.** Start a plant growing, such as a carrot top in a dish of water; make a chart and help your child keep track of how fast the stem grows; mark when the leaves come out and notice how the roots look.

✦ **Feed the birds.** Put out a bird feeder and keep a list of the different kinds of birds that come to eat; describe different birds' similarities and also how you can tell them apart.

✦ **Bring out the meteorologist in him.** Keep a weather chart with your child so that at the end of the month you can count the number of rainy, sunny, and cloudy days.

✦ **Take a nature walk.** Collect wildflowers while walking in the woods. Later try to identify them in a book about wildflowers.

✦ **Search for nature books.** Borrow books about butterflies and cocoons, dinosaurs, birds—animals that interest both you and your child. Talk about the way animals grow, where they live, how they change, and so on.

✦ **Help your child with his questions.** Listen carefully when your child asks "why" questions, and plan ways to involve him in finding answers, such as asking an expert, looking in a book, or observing together to gather evidence.

✦ **Listen and look.** Encourage your child to listen to the sounds of the woods, of the night, of the city, and then try to identify the source.

✦ **Be curious yourself.** Wonder how moss can grow on a tree or on cement without any dirt; what makes wind? Make up silly science questions together.

EXPLAINING AND PREDICTING

Pre-kindergartners wonder about everything, exploring and examining anything within reach. They are fascinated by their world and everything they come across. Four-year-olds are beginning to try to explain what they see, making guesses, and inventing reasons to explain "why."

FROM SCHOOL TO HOME

Your four-year-old's teacher thoughtfully guides children's interests. That's why your child will have the opportunity to, for example, talk about an injured bird brought to class and guess what it needs for food, whether or not it should go to a veterinarian, and so on. Your little scientist may also ask increasingly probing questions, looking for explanations about a caterpillar brought to class: "What does it eat? How does it change into a butterfly? How does it breathe? Is it dead when it is in the cocoon?" She's likely to explain what makes the noise in a conch shell when she holds it to her ear or guess what new colors will appear when she mixes them for an art project. And she makes guesses about which objects will float and which will sink in a pan of water.

Your child will bring lots of questions and answers home: "I know what makes the leaves in the yard turn red! But why do other leaves turn yellow in the fall?"; "The moon is following me down the sidewalk!" She'll want to dig up flowers in the garden to inspect the roots; she'll look at moss growing on a tree, feel it, and want to bring some of it into the house. She'll also become excited about the first snowfall and want to explore the flakes up close.

IT'S YOUR TURN

To keep those good guesses coming:

+ **Examine an egg.** Cook an egg with your child and talk about how it changes as it cooks.

+ **Watch grass grow.** Together, place some grass seeds on a wet sponge and watch them sprout and grow; describe to each other what you see and guess what will happen next.

+ **Get touchy.** Provide a variety of things for your child to touch, such as cotton, silk, velvet, sandpaper, flour, sugar, water, and oil; ask her to describe how each one feels on her hands with her eyes shut and then guess what each is.

+ **Give her a glass.** Teach your child how to use a magnifying glass; encourage her to use it all around the house and outdoors, guessing how something might look magnified and then checking to find out.

+ **Start a collection.** Together collect natural items, such as stones, leaves, or seashells, and help her talk about her observations. For example, if you are collecting stones, discuss their various colors, shapes, and textures. Talk about ways they are different from each other.

+ **Color her world.** Put various food coloring tints in several glasses of water; add stalks of celery and watch the stalks change color; ask your child why she thinks this happens.

+ **Guess how your garden grows.** Write down your child's guesses about which of the seeds you planted in your garden will come up first; talk about what the plants will look like, and keep watch to see if your guesses were right.

+ **Wonder about the weather.** Let your child guess what makes a day cloudy, or what makes snow or rain.

+ **Guesses galore.** Guess with your child what will happen to the apples in the pie as it bakes, or where the ants are going when you see one on the sidewalk.

+ **Be bookish.** Borrow books from the library that show the life cycle of caterpillars, or how seeds turn into plants.

+ **Set an example.** Explain to your child as you experience the world, i.e., what plants need in order to grow, how dust balls get under the bed, what makes a sponge float, and so on.

CHAPTER 13

Social Studies

✦

Four-year-olds are very interested in families: "Who is related to me? Who is related to you? What does 'related' mean? What does it mean that Essie is my cousin?" They want to know all about family roles: "What is Daddy's job in the family? What is his job at work? What is my job in this family? Will I be a Daddy/Mommy when I grow up? What will my job be?"

In the wider community, children this age are very interested in firefighters, police officers, mail carriers, and other workers. They want to know who is in charge of them in their family, at school, in the library. They are interested in classmates who come from different cultures. For four-year-olds, social studies is about:

People and how they live together

**How the past, the land, and people
affect each other**

PEOPLE AND HOW THEY LIVE TOGETHER

Four-year-olds generally understand only what is directly within their life experience. They find it difficult to grasp what it would be like to live in a different place with different customs. And, as is true for many adults, children are often uncomfortable around people who look different or do things that seem strange.

At this age, children are beginning to look at the ways people in their community—police officers, doctors, bus drivers—contribute to their family's safety and well-being. They are interested in rules as well as routines and how they keep us safe. Preschoolers are likely to test boundaries, but they are dependent on order and conformity. They learn that we are all a community of people living together, each helping one another.

From School to Home

The diverse community in many preschool classrooms offers many ways for children to learn about other kinds of people. Your four-year-old may be interested in a new classmate who speaks a different language, and he may even learn a few words or expressions in that language. He'll start noticing physical differences among the children in his classroom: hair color, eye color, skin color, height, weight. As he plays in class, your child will explore the varying roles of family members. And perhaps he'll pretend to be a doctor examining patients. He participates in class discussions to establish the rules that make the classroom run smoothly: How many people can be at the sand table at the same time; how to know whose turn it is.

At home you may see your child line up a group of stuffed animals and point out their similarities and differences. Suddenly he'll tell you that he wants to grow up to help other people. He may also tell a younger sibling about the "no hitting" rule he learned at school or talk about how the rules in your family are made. And he'll ask to go to work with you to find out what you do.

It's Your Turn

To increase your child's understanding and appreciation of others:

✦ **Talk about your family.** Discuss the similarities of and differences in your ages, size, hair and eye color, and talents (ability to sing, draw, garden, do plumbing, work on cars or motorcycles, and so on).

✦ **Diversify his book list.** Read to your child about those who live in different parts of the world, and talk about the ways others are alike and different from you and your family.

✦ **Make a rainbow collage.** Together, cut out pictures of all types of people from catalogues or magazines and paste them into a collage of diversity.

✦ **Point out the community around you.** As the two of you go about your errands, talk with your child about the workers you see—traffic officers, store clerks, telephone repair people, and so on—and the jobs they do.

✦ **Tell a communal story.** Read stories to your child about community helpers and point out why you need all the people who work in your town.

✦ **List good works.** As you and your child go through the day, list all the people you see doing jobs that help others.

✦ **Engage in auto-shop talk.** As you go for a drive, think of and discuss all the people who might have done jobs to help make your car.

✦ **Imagine life without...** Talk with your child about what would happen if there were no people to grow food, collect garbage, or sell books and newspapers.

✦ **Have him set house rules.** Let your child and his sibling figure out how each can have a turn with the tape or CD player.

✦ **Discuss social rules.** Talk with your child about public manners. Help him understand that appropriate social behaviors such as asking permission to touch things, saying thank you, and saying goodbye rather than just walking out the door make the people he is with happy to have him visit.

✦ **Create rules for the road.** Together, make a list of rules for car trips, both for safety and for making the trip more enjoyable for everyone. (Include fun activities as well as the rules.)

✦ **Stop, go, walk, and wait.** Point out to your child the various traffic rules, and discuss what would happen if these rules were not obeyed.

HOW THE PAST, THE LAND, AND PEOPLE AFFECT ONE ANOTHER

How do people live in other places? How do people affect their environment? How does the environment affect them? These are questions four-year-olds can answer only in the most simple, concrete ways, based on their immediate experience. As in most areas of learning, it is up to their parents and teachers to lay the groundwork for future concepts and understanding.

From School to Home

Your child has many experiences in preschool that encourage her to think about how she and others affect their environment. For one thing, she can see what happens on the playground when children don't pick up their litter; then she'll take part in classroom discussions about how this affects the world. She begins to understand why she is supposed to put toys and materials away before starting new projects. She and her classmates start recycling bins for paper, leftover food, and cans. She looks at books about children living in other climates and figures out how their food, houses, and clothing might be different from her own. In terms of beginning geographic thinking, she may make a list of the furniture in a room at home and then draw a picture to show how it is arranged.

Don't be surprised when your four-year-old tells family members not to throw paper out the car window. She may also ask you to start a recycling bin for paper and cans if you have not already done so. She may wonder aloud what it would be like if your house were at the North Pole. And she'll look at a map of your city or town and ask you to point out the line that represents the road you live on.

"I use the ideas in this section with my child when he has questions about people who are different from him or who live in a different way."

IT'S YOUR TURN

You'll help open your child's eyes to the world around her when you:

✦ **Focus on the neighborhood.** To start your child thinking about "mapping," comment on the houses on your street as you walk to the bus; then help your child draw a picture of your street and the houses on it.

✦ **Make a model together.** With clay, photos, or drawings, depict a major street near you and place the buildings and stores in their correct positions.

✦ **Admire the landscaping.** On a walk, point out the ways neighbors have planted flowers and bushes to make their front yards look more beautiful; the ways in which they are enhancing their environment.

✦ **Appreciate your natural resources.** Visit a lake or park in your community and talk about how different your city would be if the lake or park were not there; what kinds of things can you do because the lake or the park is near you?

✦ **Talk trash.** Discuss what it would be like if everyone threw their garbage on the ground instead of taking it to a waste bin.

✦ **Grab the garbage.** Carry a plastic bag with you when you walk in the woods, and pick up any trash you see along the way.

✦ **Rave about recycling.** Help your child understand the important reasons for recycling as you have her help you separate your trash into appropriate containers.

✦ **...and about re-using.** Also talk about fixing broken toys rather than throwing them away.

✦ **Seasonal chat.** Talk with your child about how the seasons change, what you wear in different seasons, or varying ways that you can play outside as the seasons change.

✦ **Street history.** Begin discussion with your child about what your street might have been before the street was paved and the houses built. What happened to the animals that lived there, and the plants and trees?

✦ **Street work.** Think about the kinds of jobs the people who live on your street have. Would they be able to have these jobs if they lived somewhere else? For example, a taxi driver might not have a job if he lived far away from the city.

CHAPTER 14

The Arts

✦

Children have numerous opportunities to try out a variety of art materials and forms in preschool and child care programs. They are encouraged to paint at the easel and to explore a variety of art materials such as chalk, crayons, markers, water colors, finger paint, clay, and play dough. Children are provided multiple opportunities to sing, play musical instruments, act out stories, dance, and pretend in many different ways. These artistic activities allow children to express their joy and enthusiasm and explore their reactions to the world around them. They also help them develop their small and large motor skills. Four-year-olds' progress in the arts can be seen through their:

Artistic expression

Artistic appreciation

ARTISTIC EXPRESSION

Children are excited about and able to express themselves with the various art forms available to them in preschool. They love to paint and use magic markers, dance and sing, act out stories, and express ideas. The arts provide four-year-olds with an outlet for their energy and imagination as well as a chance to learn new skills. All children will not be equally captivated by or skilled in each of the artistic forms, but they will learn that there are many ways to express their creativity and ideas. What's important is that they are being exposed to creative processes without pressure to produce a specific product.

FROM SCHOOL TO HOME

Preschool is a wonderful place to foster creative expression. Your four-year-old explores a variety of materials to express his creative impulses. He paints with a variety of tools such as a cotton swab, a straw, leaves, hair rollers, a toy car making tracks through a splash of paint, or his fingers. He messes about with play dough, rolling, squashing, and poking it; then he uses implements, such as cookie cutters, rolling pins, sticks, or pipe cleaners, to create new dough shapes and forms. He may draw with markers while listening to music. And he sings songs to tell a story, explore numbers, play with rhyming words, express feelings, and accompany his dancing or finger motions. He is encouraged to use rhythm sticks, triangles, and other percussion instruments to explore rhythm, beat, and tempo.

At home, your child has explored various art forms for some time. He is now at the stage where he'll try to create representational drawings of people, animals, or houses. He'll dance to music he hears on a tape, a CD, or the radio. He'll beat out a rhythm with a spoon on the table or try out an older brother's drum set. You'll hear him sing new songs or perform finger plays or act out a story he's learned at school.

"We love the arts section. And you don't have to spend a lot of money to do these things!"

IT'S YOUR TURN

To encourage and promote your child's creative instincts:

✦ **Foster his originality.** Keep crayons, markers, stickers, tape, paste, and "beautiful junk" where your child can readily use them when he feels the urge to create.

✦ **Paint with feeling.** With finger paint or shaving cream on paper, paint together to music, swirl the sounds of spring, or create your emotions—happiness, sadness, fear, anger.

✦ **Share your childhood songs.** Teach your child some songs you sang at school or camp.

✦ **...and have him share his.** Ask your child to teach you his new school songs; then sing them with him in the car or while waiting in line.

✦ **Take time to rhyme.** Make up rhyming songs or sing well-known songs, such as "The Name Game" ("banana fanna").

✦ **Sing from a songbook.** Ask your child's teacher for a children's music book that might include songs your child has sung at school as well as other songs you could sing together.

✦ **Step lively!** With your child, dance in your living room to a variety of recorded music, trying different rhythms, tempos, and moods.

✦ **Get percussive.** Make shaker instruments with tubes, jars, and boxes; decorate them together; then play them together.

✦ **Prepare for a puppet show.** Turn a large cardboard carton into a puppet theater, and encourage your child to create stories using hand or finger puppets.

✦ **Make play dough.** Mix together 2 c flour, 1 c salt, 1/2 c water and add food coloring; "mold" as many things as either of you can think of, or just have fun rolling and squeezing it.

✦ **Show him you care.** Express interest in the work your child does and the art objects he makes.

ARTISTIC APPRECIATION

It is important that children notice and appreciate the artistic expressions of others. One way four-year-olds learn to do this is when the adults in their lives point out and discuss with them the illustrators of favorite picture books. There are many art forms children might not recognize as art, for example, the magician who performs at their school or the clown at the shopping mall. Art and expressions of artists' feelings and stories are all around children's lives. Preschoolers are ready to appreciate these artistic expressions.

FROM SCHOOL TO HOME

Your four-year-old is an audience for all sorts of art forms at school. She looks at drawings in picture books and talks about the way artists illustrate a scene or a feeling. She listens to music and then tells the story she thinks the composer is trying to express. Her classmates' work also draws her appreciation: She may enjoy a peer's clay sculpture or Lego construction, delight in a friend's imitation of a dinosaur, or applaud an improvised dance or a play about taking turns. She also appreciates the sounds of a visiting violinist or the skill of a guest painting teacher.

When you read to your child at home, she may point out the way the illustrator drew the pictures. She'll tell you about a performer who visited her class. Your child will also clap for you when you, for example, play a favorite piece on the piano, and she'll tell a sibling what a good job he or she did in making a block design.

IT'S YOUR TURN

To encourage your young art enthusiast:

✦ **Focus on the pictures.** Talk about the illustrations in books as you read to your child; ask what she likes about them or how she thinks they might be drawn differently.

✦ **Peruse pretty patterns.** Look at the pattern on your dishes and try to imagine who designed it and how that person transferred the artistic idea onto the dishes.

✦ **Admire floral arrangements.** Look at the flower gardens in the city park and think about the people who planted them; try to figure out if the gardens were planned with a particular design in mind.

✦ **Marvel at a museum's magic.** Go to a children's museum with your child and talk about the display and how someone planned the exhibits to look a certain way.

✦ **Move her with your music.** Sing or play the piano, and ask your child whether the song seems sad or happy, whether it makes her want to gallop or sway, and so on.

✦ **Concentrate on children's music.** Listen together and try to pick out the different instruments being played.

✦ **See *The Sound of Music***—or another movie musical—and talk about how the music helped to tell the story.

✦ **Watch body language.** Take your child to a dance recital, and ask her what the dancers are trying to express with their movements.

✦ **Clowning around.** Watch the clown at a circus or the flute player in the mall and think about the skills they have developed to do their act.

✦ **Learning lines.** As you watch television together think about how the actors have to learn their parts.

✦ **Art all around.** Look for a craft fair and investigate the way the artisans are able to execute their particular crafts.

CHAPTER 15

Physical Development and Health

✦

Children learn by doing. Since so much of what they do is highly active and physical, it follows that children's physical development and the health of their bodies are very important to their mental development. Four-year-olds are enthusiastic in both attitude and action. Everything they do is exaggerated and exuberant—and physical. They love to run fast, climb high, gallop, jump, and hop. They also talk fast, look everywhere, and explore avidly.

It is essential that children this age have outlets to express and use this high-energy stage in their development. They need outdoor play space where there is equipment for climbing, running, and tricycling as well as free rein to shout out loud. Their ability to move broadly is complemented by their increasing small-muscle abilities, which they use for cutting, solving puzzles, and mastering self-help skills. Children's physical development is seen in three areas:

Large-muscle development

Small-muscle development

Personal health and safety/self-help skills

LARGE-MUSCLE DEVELOPMENT

At this age children expend a lot of energy through large movement. They do this by playing outside, participating in circle games, engaging in creative-movement activities, throwing, catching, running through an obstacle course, and learning to stop and turn corners on their tricycles. They love skill games but are impatient with group games when they have to wait their turn. They are eager to participate and have fun.

FROM SCHOOL TO HOME

Your four-year-old is constantly on the move in preschool. He plays a variety of group and circle games that involve large-muscle skills, such as stretching, bending, galloping, hopping, or following the leader. He has the chance to develop specific movement skills, such as hitting targets with a bean bag, kicking a large ball in an intended direction, managing a see-saw or swing, climbing on a jungle gym, and climbing the ladder on a slide. He also participates in varied creative-movement activities that help develop his imagination, motor skills, and spirit of cooperative play. He creates a variety of bodily movements to music and acts out stories about being an elephant or a monkey or a rabbit.

Your active child will go out in your yard and run, run, run! He'll want to ride his tricycle, even when it is raining outside. He'll ask a family member to play ball with him and want to go to the school playground on Saturday. And he'll show off his increasing motor skills, such as how high or far he can jump, how fast he can run, and how many times he can hop on one foot.

It's Your Turn

Hone your child's physical skills when you:

✦ **Give him room to move.** Make sure your child has outdoor time at least several times a week.

✦ **Go for a super-stroll.** While you take a walk with your child, jump, hop, take extra-long steps, take tiny steps, march, and see who can walk fastest and slowest.

✦ **Hit the playground!** Go several times a month so he can run, climb, crawl, slide, swing, and balance.

✦ **Play physical games**—such as "Simon Says" and "Follow the Leader," and make up your own games as well.

✦ **Toss a beanbag.** Take turns throwing one into a bucket or at a target.

✦ **Play catch.** Use that beanbag again or a large rubber ball.

✦ **...and follow the bouncing ball.** Use balloons or a tennis ball to throw, catch, toss in the air, and chase around. Use big balls and small balls to practice bouncing, throwing, catching, kicking, and batting.

✦ **Take the stairs together.** Make a point of walking up stairs rather than using elevators or escalators. This will do *both* of your bodies some good.

✦ **Dance up a storm.** Use crepe paper streamers or scarves to inspire creative movement.

✦ **Go fly a kite.** There is little that is more exciting, captivating, and peaceful than flying a kite together.

✦ **Get physical.** Do physical chores together such as raking leaves, sweeping the floor, making the bed, carrying the laundry up the stairs.

SMALL-MUSCLE DEVELOPMENT

In addition to large-muscle activities, four-year-olds are also making great strides in the development of their small-motor or hand-muscle skills. They are able to use art materials, such as brushes, scissors, paste, and tape, much more successfully than they could a year ago. They are skillful at using Legos, peg boards, and other construction materials. They can manipulate smaller puzzle pieces and are able to string beads with ease. They are also gaining greater competence in self-help skills, such as buttoning and zipping their clothing, and pouring juice.

From School to Home

In school, your child develops finger control using manipulatives, such as pattern blocks, peg boards, puzzles, beads, Duplos, Legos, and Cuisinaire rods. She practices using hand tools, such as a stapler, scissors, hole-puncher, hammer, saw, brushes, pencils, and markers. She pulls off and pushes on marker caps, twists paste-jar caps off and on, fastens together and takes apart pop beads, builds interlocking train tracks, puts on dress-up costumes, and manages snaps and buttons on her outerwear. Your creative preschooler also develops finger control through a variety of finger plays as well as songs accompanied by hand movements.

At home your busy child will want to take off the cover of the applesauce jar and put the key into the front door lock and try to turn it. She'll practice buttoning and zipping her clothes as well as lacing and unlacing her shoes as she gets dressed. And now she'll squeeze toothpaste onto her toothbrush.

"Just as my child has, I've learned so much by following the tips in this book. And my daughter feels like such a big girl when we do the activities where I have her help me with things."

IT'S YOUR TURN

To help those busy little fingers:

+ **Encourage finger fun.** Provide small-muscle materials for your child, such as beads to string, color cubes and pattern blocks with which to build and make designs, peg boards, plus Legos, bristle blocks, Duplos and other construction toys.

+ **...and art supplies** such as blunt scissors to cut out strips for weaving or pictures for pasting.

+ **...and water colors and markers** for finger and wrist action while creating.

+ **Collectively create collages.** Use flour paste and household items, such as yarn, rick-rack, ribbon, pipe cleaners, spaghetti or macaroni, colored wrapping paper, leaves, and sticks, to craft beautiful designs on paper.

+ **Decorate!** Make holiday decorations together, such as paper chains, place mats woven from strips of colored construction paper, and paper doilies decorated with cut-out hearts.

+ **Prepare her to print.** Set up printing projects using ink pads and rubber stamps, sponges, carved potato stamps, and so on.

+ **Bring out the chef in her.** Let your child help you prepare foods by scraping carrots, spreading peanut butter on bread, stirring pudding, whisking eggs, and so on.

+ **...and bake!** Let her measure out the dry ingredients for cookies, or mix the pancake batter.

+ **...and sew!** Create your own sewing cards with laces to encourage finger control.

+ **Play cards.** Try games such as "Concentration," in which she has to pick up and turn over cards, or games such as "Old Maid," "Go Fish," or "Crazy Eights," in which she must hold cards in her hand and place cards on the table in piles.

+ **Feed the birds.** Make bird feeders together by stringing suet or popcorn or by spreading honey on pine cones.

PERSONAL HEALTH AND SAFETY/SELF-HELP SKILLS

Four-year-olds love to help during daily routines. They can be quite determined about dressing themselves, even insisting on picking out their own clothes. They practice buttoning and unbuttoning, zipping zippers, or lacing shoes for long periods of time. They can feed themselves without spills and love to pour their own juice or help themselves from serving dishes. In addition, pre-kindergartners can take care of most of their bathroom routines: They can brush their own teeth and dry their own hands; they like to wash themselves in the bathtub. They still need adult supervision, however, because they are easily distracted and may forget to finish what they start.

FROM SCHOOL TO HOME

Preschool teachers offer four-year-olds plenty of opportunities to take care of themselves. Your child puts on his own paint smock and outerwear. At school he goes to the bathroom by himself and washes and dries his hands with no help after using the toilet and before snack time. He learns about and enjoys a variety of healthful snack foods, such as raisins, carrot sticks, dried fruit, raw string beans, sliced apples, and yogurt. And he uses safety rules on the playground, such as standing back from the swings or going up the slide ladder one rung at a time.

Your increasingly self-sufficient four-year-old will now insist on zipping his own jacket, snapping fasteners, and buttoning his shirt or coat. He will no longer ask you for help when going to the toilet, and he'll wash his hands before meals and after toileting, as he does in school. Watch him get undressed for bed and brush his teeth by himself. And he'll now explain safety rules to you, such as looking both ways for cars when crossing the street, stopping at red lights, or telling a police officer his address should he become lost.

IT'S YOUR TURN

To help your child help himself:

+ **Teach hygiene by example.** Model good habits by washing your hands before eating or cooking and after using the bathroom.

+ **Encourage him to handle self-care.** Show your child how to wash in the bathtub, how to brush his teeth thoroughly, and how to wash his hands so they are clean.

+ **Teach sneezing etiquette.** Help your child with proper health practices, such as covering his mouth when he sneezes and throwing used tissues in the wastebasket; demonstrate these practices yourself.

+ **Talk nutrition.** Explain why you serve certain foods and not others, that the foods taste good as well as help your child to grow and be healthy. Discuss and maybe even chart the food groups, such as vegetables, fruits, whole grains, and dairy products, and what you like to eat from them. In this way you'll help him learn that nutrition and taste are both important to good eating.

+ **Snack on the healthy stuff.** Have cut-up pieces of carrots, celery, apples, cheese, and oranges available for snacks.

+ **Prepare pourables.** Put juice and milk into small pitchers so your child can pour his own drinks.

+ **Show him how to sop it up.** Teach your child how to clean up his own spills.

+ **Let him dress solo.** Leave enough time when getting ready to go out for your child to button his own coat, zip his own pants, and put on his own socks and shoes.

+ **Talk safety.** Discuss safety rules, such as waiting at street corners for an adult to help him cross, holding hands when in a crowded place, using car seats, and making sure everyone buckles up before you start the car.

+ **...and helmets.** Encourage wearing a helmet when he rides his trike or two-wheeler with training wheels.

+ **...and safe driving.** Talk about the rules of the road when you chauffeur him around.

Winning Ways to Learn
for 5-Year-Olds

CHAPTER 16

Personal and Social Development

✦

Confident kindergartners can begin to learn letters, numbers, reading, and writing. They can thrive in a classroom where they also learn how to cooperate, solve problems, and interact with others. In turn, the way they relate to other children and to their teachers plays an important part in their overall school success. For these reasons both personal and social development represent a vital component of learning. Children's growth in this area can be viewed through their:

Self-concept and self-control

Approach to learning

Interactions with others

SELF-CONCEPT AND SELF-CONTROL

A child who has a strong self-concept feels good about himself. His confidence is strengthened by opportunities to be independent, take responsibility, and follow his parents' and teachers' guidance about living alongside others. A kindergartner's sense of self develops as he has positive experiences in groups of familiar children and adults. His self-control increases as he follows classroom rules, learns how games are played, follows daily schedules, and understands how to use and take care of the materials he needs. These experiences help a five-year-old learn that he is liked by others and that he has something of value to contribute to the group.

FROM SCHOOL TO HOME

Your kindergartner's teacher encourages him to develop confidence and competence in many ways. Through sharing a story with his classmates during Circle Time, collecting materials for a project and then using them to work independently, and even checking the job chart and doing the assigned job, his sense of self deepens and expands. Each time he stops an activity when the bell rings, when he hears his name called, or when he realizes how many children can play at a particular activity center and then, when there is not room, chooses another center, his ability to exercise self-control is flexed and strengthened.

He brings these skills home when he participates in family discussions comfortably and meaningfully. Suddenly he is able to tie his shoes and demonstrate other new skills. When he makes a mistake, he tries again, without the frustration you may have seen a few short months ago. He may, for the first time, offer to help with family projects or chores and then check off the jobs he completes on a chart. And he may begin to remember, without your prompting him, to say *please* and *thank you* when appropriate.

"I like the idea of helping children to understand a schedule or agenda. This will help them later on in school, too."

IT'S YOUR TURN

To help your child make the most of what he's gained from school:

✦ **Talk and play with your child.** By showing him that you enjoy his company, you will help him enjoy and appreciate himself.

✦ **Give him a job.** Simple household tasks, such as setting or clearing the table for meals, making his own bed, feeding the family pet, or putting away his clean laundry, will give him a sense of his own responsibility and importance.

✦ **Then give him a more complicated job.** Let your child help you prepare lunch or dinner by tossing the salad, measuring and pouring the ingredients for the cookies you are baking, or putting decorations on a cake.

✦ **Create a chart together.** Ask your child to keep track of the jobs he has completed each day. He'll gain a sense of mastery as he charts and sees clearly all that he has accomplished.

✦ **Make a weekly plan.** Together, draft a weekly schedule of times and events, underlining items that are different from his usual routine. Children feel safer and begin to understand the order of things when they have a schedule to follow.

✦ **Watch him; listen to him; praise him.** When you show appreciation and interest in your child's growing skills and interests, you bolster his self-esteem and encourage further activity.

✦ **Let your child make reasonable choices and decisions,** such as which shirt to wear to school, what story to read at bedtime, or what kind of fruit to have at snack time. In this way you encourage his independent thinking.

✦ **Make his things available to him.** You invite independent action when you store your child's toys, games, books, and art materials where he can get them out and put them away on his own.

✦ **Teach him about order**—how to finish one thing and put it away before getting out another.

✦ **...and about public rules**—for visiting places such as the library or the grocery store.

✦ **...and about social graces.** Help your child learn appropriate behaviors when visiting in friends' homes, such as not touching things without asking or not going into rooms without an invitation. Manners such as these help make the people you are visiting and your child more relaxed. Friends are happy to welcome you and your child into their home.

✦ **Watch TV together.** Good programs, such as *Sesame Street*, offer a chance to share valuable messages. Jointly make a list of the lessons seen on a show and discuss them.

APPROACH TO LEARNING

Children approach learning in a variety of ways; some may be watchers, others listeners, doers, or thinkers. Regardless of *how* they learn, most five-year-olds are eager and excited about the fresh challenges that kindergarten has to offer, especially when activities involve moving, talking, feeling, and creating, rather than long periods of sitting, listening, and writing.

Your child is likely to have several favorite activities, but, with some encouragement, she will try new ones as well. As with most kindergartners, she may become frustrated or give up when she encounters a difficult problem, such as putting a roof on a block building, folding paper a certain way, or drawing a particular animal. But with help and encouragement she's apt to experiment with problem-solving and stick with a challenge until a solution is found. In this way she begins to learn an important concept: that making mistakes is part of learning.

FROM SCHOOL TO HOME

In school your child's teacher creates an environment of wonder. Your child gets excited when she observes a new shell or rock collection on the discovery table. She has the opportunity to study pictures of different buildings and try to build one of them with blocks, or to look at books in the book corner to find answers to questions. The school routine encourages your child to do her daily jobs, such as feed the classroom hamster or record the outside temperature. And when she can't figure out how to complete a puzzle, she knows she can go to her teacher for help.

The classroom focus and excitement stays with her as your child hurries home to have you read her a book just checked out of the library. On the way home, however, she may stop briefly to wonder about an intriguing insect crawling on the ground. You'll probably notice that she is interested in new topics and activities, and her interest in them may translate into projects that she sticks with for longer and longer periods of time. Suddenly she sees things to do or create with in an assortment of junk or found materials (such as wrapping paper, interesting boxes, bits of yarn or ribbon, buttons, bottle caps, bread tags, stickers, labels, colored construction paper, and so on)—cutting, pasting, folding, and stacking in new ways. And now she listens to and asks questions about stories told by family members.

IT'S YOUR TURN

To nurture your child's growing sense of discovery:

✦ **Display your own wonder.** Set an example for your child by being curious about things you see when out on a walk and noticing things that are happening around you.

✦ **Ask your child questions.** When you question her about things that interest her, you help her learn how to recall events that have happened and express what she thought about them.

✦ **Turn your answers into further exploration.** For example, when your child asks what happens to snow when it melts (or ice when it gets warm), suggest gathering a cup of snow (or a bowl of ice cubes) to leave indoors and watching what happens to it. Or when she asks how a caterpillar turns into a butterfly, suggest finding a book at the library that explains this process.

✦ **Keep the challenges coming.** Engage your child in playing new games, reading a variety of books, or planning new activities to keep her active mind stimulated and reaching for more.

✦ **Teach her to think twice.** Encourage your child to think of more than one way to do things, such as coming up with two ways to mix eggs or different ways to walk from home to the park.

✦ **Help your child take the next step.** Suggest ways she can extend projects she has started, such as adding a new part to a block building, bringing a different color into her drawing, using paste to attach a cut-out to a background, or adding a briefcase to her dress-up for "going to work."

✦ **Encourage "stick-to-itiveness."** Help your child stay with activities for longer periods of time by joining her when she seems to be tiring and talking with her about what she is doing or creating.

✦ **Teach your child how to master new skills:** cutting out cookie dough, folding napkins for dinner in a new way, using stickers on cards to make place cards for a special meal.

✦ **Model patience.** When you wait for your child to get her own ideas in order and give her time to express them, she learns that her ideas are important enough to warrant your unhurried attention.

✦ **Share a family flick.** Watch one of your child's favorite home videos together, and help her make the popcorn. In this way you encourage sharing, communication, and the fun of taking pleasure in the same things.

✦ **Have her be teacher for a day.** Play school with your child, letting her be the teacher so she can explain to you what you need to learn.

INTERACTIONS WITH OTHERS

Most five-year-olds are social beings. They love being with other children and adults they know, like, and trust. Kindergartners are very interested in the idea of friendship and often have one or two favorite friends — children they know quite well. Some five-year-olds are very caring and understanding toward other children while others will need some gentle guidance about how to act this way. Children this age may need help and encouragement getting acquainted with new friends.

You may notice that your child sometimes acts without thinking when a social conflict arises. He may say or do things he doesn't really mean. He is just beginning to learn how to deal with disagreements and arguments by talking, discussing a compromise, and coming to an agreement. But like most kindergartners, he probably cannot do this on his own. With gentle help—and many repetitions—he will gradually learn these social skills.

FROM SCHOOL TO HOME

The kindergarten teacher provides varied opportunities for your child to interact with others. He can play in the block area, the dress-up area, or at the water table with two or three other children. In these situations he talks, listens, and helps solve problems, sometimes giving ideas and sometimes using the ideas of others. He is also learning to ask for help when another child wants to play with the same blocks he is using. He may have the opportunity to listen to a story told by a friend about a sad event (the death of a pet hamster) and show his capacity for sympathy by giving a hug. He learns to use words, such as, "I don't like it when you do that, because it makes me mad," instead of hitting or pushing. At school, he is learning to talk to adults with comfort and ease.

Your sociable child will then come home and ask to invite a friend over to play. He may also ask to take a special book to school to show a friend, or take a postcard from Grandma to show the teacher. He has learned that he can come to you for help when he has a disagreement with a sibling. And he now knows that he should tell you when he is angry at you rather than shouting and running to his room.

IT'S YOUR TURN

To help your child sharpen social skills:

✦ **Plan a playdate.** Show interest in your child's friendships by arranging for a special pal to come over.

✦ **Teach him to care.** Encourage your child to help others — to show sympathy when a friend is hurt or sad by staying with him, offering to help, or possibly suggesting something fun to do together.

✦ **Make manners matter.** Remind him that saying *please* and *thank you* and *good morning* or *goodnight* when appropriate is important to friends and family.

✦ **Let him create a social event.** Help your child think of something that would be fun for him and several friends, such as going to the zoo or a playground, and arrange for it to happen.

✦ **Play games.** Your child will learn about rules and how to handle winning and losing when family members play games together and have fun doing it.

✦ **Read and discuss books about friendship.** Stories that include friends doing things together, working out problems, and planning activities will help your child with his own social interactions. Great books that promote buddyhood: *Charlotte's Web* by E. B. White, the George and Martha series of books by James Marshall, and *Yoko* by Rosemary Wells.

✦ **Ask for an answer.** Encourage your child to answer questions or respond when someone says something to him.

✦ **Practice conflict resolution.** Teach your child what to do when a problem with a peer arises: For example, he can walk away, get help from an adult, or tell the other person how he feels.

✦ **Talk over upsets when they are over.** After he has calmed down from being upset, help your child think about other ways of reacting, such as talking about the problem, not yelling, or even counting to 10 before doing anything. Make a plan for the next time he is angry and help him follow it.

✦ **Model emotionally sound behavior.** React calmly to your own problems; express your feelings in words when you become angry and try to explain why you are upset; and settle conflicts peacefully.

✦ **Talk about what you see.** Select television programs that you feel have educational value and discuss how the characters in the program get along and help one another. Limiting the amount of television watching is important for young children. If, by chance, your child sees violence on television or a video, talk with him about what happens when people do these kinds of things.

CHAPTER 17

Language and Literacy

✦

They may not yet be reading or writing on their own, but five-year-olds have developed impressive language skills. To make the leap to literacy, they must experience literature as something exciting and compelling. They must also have a wide enough command of letters, sounds, and vocabulary so that words in print will have meaning for them. In this way they get closer and closer to standard forms of language as they become older and more experienced. Their progress can be seen in:

Listening and speaking

Literature and reading

Writing

LISTENING AND SPEAKING

Kindergartners love to talk and be listened to. They listen with relish when they are interested in what is being said. They are able to focus attention on casual conversations, stories read aloud, television, videos, and spoken directions. Most of what they say is clear, but it is not unusual for them to continue mispronouncing a few sounds. They are learning many new words and they love to test them out. Making up words or silly rhymes and listening to the sound of them as they repeat them over and over is something most children of this age greatly enjoy.

FROM SCHOOL TO HOME

Her teacher and class environment offer your kindergartner a wealth of language experience. She learns to listen to stories for increasingly longer periods of time, and her comprehension grows. She learns to retell a story just read to the class using puppets or a flannel board. She regularly looks at and listens to other children telling stories during Circle Time or class discussions. In turn, your child works to speak clearly so everyone can understand. She listens to and follows the directions about snack time, recess, or clean-up.

As in school, your child is willing and able to pay attention to others while stories are told at home at the dinner table. She also participates in mealtime chats by telling you what happened at school, even if it is a few days later. She may tell a joke to the family and laugh uproariously, although her audience may not understand what the joke is about or what makes it funny. And she can listen to a story on tape or the radio and then tell you all about it. She easily responds to your cues for getting ready for school. Your wonderful five-year-old can also answer the phone, speaking clearly and answering questions appropriately.

"It's been difficult for me to get feedback about school from my child, but many of these ideas have helped."

IT'S YOUR TURN

To encourage your child's verbal give-and-take:

✦ **Converse with her, often!** Take turns listening and talking so your child has the opportunity to listen with understanding and then respond meaningfully.

✦ **Talk *to* her.** Let her know she's a part of family discussions by talking directly to her.

✦ **Play word games,** in which you and your child create rhymes or discover what the other is looking at by asking questions and guessing from the clues.

✦ **...and listening–concentration games,** such as "Simon Says" or "In my bag I packed a..."

✦ **Make reading a creative guessing game.** When you ask your child to guess what a book's character will do next or to make up a different ending, you promote her imaginative thinking.

✦ **Give multi-part directions.** Offer your child clear directions consisting of several steps, and then ask her to repeat them before she carries them out.

✦ **Train her in telephone talk.** Teach your child telephone manners (the right way to say hello, how to respond to the caller's questions), and let her answer the phone.

✦ **Tell chain tales**. Make up stories together where your child listens to your part, adds on her part, and then listens to you again, and so on. This will help develop both her memory and her imagination.

✦ **Tell a true story together.** Ask your child to help you tell the rest of the family about who you saw at the store or about a funny thing that happened on the way to school today.

✦ **Listen to nature's sounds together:** the wind, rustling leaves, insects' calls; help your child identify birds by their songs.

✦ **Tape the sounds of life**—both inside and outside your home. Play them for your child and ask her to identify the sounds; then ask her to make a tape of sounds for you to identify.

✦ **Hear the music.** Discuss the different sounds and the various rhythms, and even dance to the music. By doing this you will help your child hear the differences among a variety of sounds, respond to different kinds of rhythms, and learn to interpret the messages in music.

✦ **Sing, recite, and rhyme.** Take every opportunity to sing songs together, recite poems, and make up rhymes. This will train your child's ear for the rhythm of words and language.

✦ **Script chats.** Engage in pretend conversations with your child. The goal: to help her learn to respond meaningfully when people ask her questions, give her compliments, or ask her to do things.

LITERATURE AND READING

Books: They are—or should be—among young children's favorite things. Kindergartners love to be read to and will listen to stories they enjoy for long periods of time (20 minutes or more). They also explore books on their own, looking at the pictures, "reading" them to dolls or a friend, and taking books with them on car trips to pass the time. Five-year-olds often want to be actively involved in the stories, asking questions, guessing what will happen next, or making up different endings.

After being read a story your child should be able, with your encouragement, to retell it in his own words, answer questions about what happened, name characters, and even identify the problem presented in the story. He's likely to realize that reading means looking at words on a page and saying the words out loud. He may even be able to read a few words: his name, family members' names, food labels, simple words, such as *cat* and *dog*, or neighborhood signs, such as *STOP*, *WALK*, or *McDonald's*.

FROM SCHOOL TO HOME

A kindergarten teacher makes sure that reading, letters, sounds, and books are a big part of your child's school experience. The teacher establishes regular story times, during which the children listen to and discuss many different types of stories. Your child may also spend time in the "listening center," hearing stories on tapes and following along in a book. He may use puppets to retell a favorite story. There will be plenty of books, from which he can choose favorites by looking at covers or picking out words in the titles. He can use information from these books to find out the name of an insect found on the playground or where a particularly scary-looking dinosaur used to live. And there's plenty more to read in the classroom, such as signs that say *EXIT*, *DOOR*, and *FISH*.

At home, your child will want a story or two (or more!) read every night at bedtime and will ask to go to the library to take out favorite books. He may begin to memorize stories and "read" them to you, or guess about what will happen next in a new story. Signs, labels, notes, and words on television will prompt him to ask, "What does that say?"

IT'S YOUR TURN

Study after study reveals that reading with your child is essential for building knowledge that leads to success in learning. To foster your child's love of reading:

+ **Go to the library.** Help your child pick out and borrow a variety of books.

+ **Ask about what you read.** Stop in the middle of reading a story and ask, "What do you think will happen next?"

+ **Talk about the tale.** Discuss what happened in a story, what he liked about it, and, if there were parts he didn't like, why that was so.

+ **Let him "read" to you.** He'll feel important and begin to understand that he is beginning to read.

+ **Make a "Words I Can Read" list together.** Post it on the refrigerator and add to it when your child recognizes a new word.

+ **Keep a word-card file.** Include words your child wants to read, adding new cards as he learns new words. He can select specific word-cards from the file when he wants to copy a word or practice sounding out a special new word.

+ **Use books to enhance other activities.** For example, watch what your child is building with blocks and encourage him to build in more detail by referring to pictures in a book. If he's building a castle, look for a book that contains pictures of castles, and try to figure out together how to add a tower or a drawbridge.

+ **Read alone, together.** Have a few minutes of quiet time, maybe after dinner, when you and your child each look at your own book. As you model your appreciation of solo reading, you'll encourage your child's independent enjoyment of books.

+ **Act out the stories you read.** You and your child can each pretend to be one of the characters and say the words that go along with the story in the book.

+ **Tune in to a tape.** Listen with your child to a children's book on tape and turn the pages in the accompanying book as the story unfolds.

+ **Read him slice-of-life stories.** Choose some books that mirror events currently happening in your child's life—the death of a pet, a visit to the dentist, a sleep-over at a friend's house.

+ **Create a reading routine.** Set a special time to read to your child every day, such as right after dinner or when he is settled in bed for the night.

+ **Let him snooze with a story.** Record a story tape yourself, and, at your child's bedtime, play it at very low volume so he can fall asleep to the soothing words. (This should not be a substitute for reading stories together.)

+ **Read, read, and read some more,** to your child, of course!

WRITING

Your kindergartner is beginning to realize that printed words have meaning and that writing is a powerful way to communicate with other people. She's probably very interested in writing notes, making signs, and "writing" original stories. Although she may not know how to make all the letters in the "correct" way or how to spell, she is learning the conventions of writing by trial and error, much the way she learned to walk and talk. Her early attempts at writing might include dictating to you while you write, scribbling and telling you what the message says, writing a string of disconnected letters that has meaning only to her, or even trying to do some phonetic spelling. Gradually she'll want to copy words, ask you to spell words for her to write, and sound out words.

FROM SCHOOL TO HOME

In school your child may draw picture stories in journals, adding scribble writing, letter strings, or a few phonetically spelled words (called "invented" or "temporary" spelling). She may recite words that go along with the pictures she has drawn, asking her teacher to write the words for her. She probably writes her name or the beginning letters of her name on her artwork and has learned to use a computer, typewriter, or letter stamps to write her name, make a sign, or print words to go along with a drawing. And she can copy words from books, picture dictionaries, and labels around the room.

On the door of her bedroom, there may be a sign she has made that reads "This is _____'s Room." She'll take advantage of other writing opportunities at home, such as adding a scribble to your shopping list to remind you to get ice cream, pretend-writing a message to send to a friend or family member, or writing her name on a letter you are sending to her grandparent.

"This book sends a clear message about what parents should expect of kindergartners at home."

IT'S YOUR TURN

You encourage your child's writing when you:

+ **Take dictation.** Offer to help add a story to your child's drawings by writing down the words she tells you. Saying stories is an important precursor to writing them.

+ **Make a word box.** Fill it with written words your child says she wants to use in her writing (*Mommy*, *Daddy*, *Grandma*, *thank you*, *I love you*, *dinosaur*, *lizard*, and so on).

+ **Spell it out.** As your child writes a message or a story, spell the words as she asks for them.

+ **Use signs.** Encourage your child to make a sign for the door of her bedroom or other rooms in the house, or a list of contents to tape to her shelves or drawers.

+ **Make chalk talk.** Mount a chalk board on a wall in the kitchen and encourage your child to draw her ideas, write her name or those of her family or friends, or just write letters of the alphabet.

+ **Create a writing center.** Set up a space for your child near where you spend a lot of time in the house. Keep it stocked with paper, pencils, envelopes, a date stamp, and her card file of words she knows. Every once in a while add a surprise of a new colored ink pen or marker or interesting paper for her to discover and use.

+ **Write love letters.** Help her put on paper a simple message to send to her grandparents—an affectionate phrase, a joke, or even a picture of herself doing something.

+ **Stock note cards.** Keep stickers and note paper handy so your child can begin to write thank-you notes to friends and relatives when they send a present or call on a special day.

+ **And help your child make greeting cards**—to send to relatives or friends on their special days or on holidays. (Have stickers, markers, glitter, and glue handy for inspiration.)

+ **Let her put her family in their place.** Together, make name cards for family members, and have your child place them where she wants people to sit at dinner or during a home-video showing.

+ **Let her list munchies.** Encourage your child to add items to your grocery shopping list using her own symbols or letters.

+ **With love from...** Ask your child to write her name at the end of a letter you are writing to a relative.

CHAPTER 18

Mathematical Thinking

✦

To five-year-olds math is all about matching, counting, comparing, adding, measuring, and identifying shapes. This means that children learn how to organize information, figure out problems, and explain how they got their answers or how they solved a puzzle. Mathematics for young children is seen in three categories:

Patterns and relationships

Numbers and their use

Geometry, spatial relations, and measurement

PATTERNS AND RELATIONSHIPS

Math isn't just about numbers. Much of it has to do with everyday logic, in terms of how to organize and make sense of mathematical information. For kindergartners, this means learning how to sort objects, see patterns in the world around them, make their own patterns, and put objects in order by size, height, length, weight, loudness, or other characteristics.

FROM SCHOOL TO HOME

There are many school activities that help kindergartners think about patterns and the order of things. You might see your child separate a collection of old keys by size, color, or shape, or arrange collections of objects (jars, stones, rods) from smallest to largest. His teacher will encourage him to look for patterns within the classroom and try to reproduce them on paper, as well as create his own patterns using math materials. Your kindergartner might also play computer games where the task is to see patterns and then extend them. Sometimes the class will go on "pattern walks," during which kids look for repeated sequences in buildings, fences, and nature.

Your five-year-old will bring this curiosity about patterns and sequences home. He'll notice patterns on wallpaper, on cloth, or in jewelry and tell you about them; and his coloring will evolve to making patterns on unlined paper. You may walk into his room one day to find that he has arranged his stuffed animals on the shelf from biggest to smallest. And just as he likes to arrange a stone collection by size or color, he'll probably enjoy helping sort glass, plastic, and cans into separate containers for recycling.

"I like most that these ideas are separated by subject, so that I can help my child do better in each area."

IT'S YOUR TURN

To help your child organize and differentiate:

✦ **Collect things together.** Gather groups of objects, such as buttons, bottle caps, or box tops, and sort them according to different rules. For example, have your child separate colors or opposites—bigger ones from smaller ones, old ones from like-new ones, or dark ones from light ones.

✦ **Figure out the food groups.** Talk with your child about the various food groups (fruits, dairy, veggies, etc.) and play games naming foods and guessing which groups they are from. ("I'm thinking of a round, red, food that goes on sandwiches..." "Tomato!" "...and it is a...fruit!")

✦ **Do the wash.** Let your child help sort the laundry into piles—all white, light colors, dark colors; or his clothes, your clothes, his sister's clothes, and so on.

✦ **Go on a pattern hunt**—in your child's room, in the wallpaper, on dishes, in the rug, in a wall border, on his shirt, and so on.

✦ **Play the pattern challenge.** Create patterns with pegs in a board or beads on a string and ask your child to name the pattern (red, red, yellow, red, red); then let him create a pattern for you to name; and continue.

✦ **Craft orderly art.** Together cut out various shapes from construction paper and paste all of one color on one page, all of one shape on another page, or big ones on one page and small ones on another. Hang the pages side-by-side on his bedroom wall.

✦ **Clap!** Try clapping patterns—two slow and three fast, one loud and two soft, and so on. Have your child repeat each pattern, then extend it; let him make up a clapping pattern for you to copy.

✦ **See it in the cards.** Create a set of duplicate cards (or a Lotto board and cards) using stickers or colored dots (available at drug stores or office-supply stores) in varying patterns, and play a game of finding cards that match.

✦ **Arrange his stuff.** Encourage your child to arrange his collection of shells, toy cars, or stuffed animals into groupings using different rules that you make up together.

✦ **Work puzzles together.** As you solve jigsaw puzzles, talk about why you picked out a particular piece to try by explaining that you matched the shape or the design.

NUMBERS AND THEIR USE

At around age five children see numbers in a new way. They begin to understand that the things they have been counting relate to quantity. Numbers take shape as tools for solving problems. They might report that 6 people were absent from school, or that they saw 12 ducks at the pond. Around this time children begin to use words to explain mathematical ideas and begin to grasp the meaning of concepts such as *more* and *less*. Most kindergartners know how to recite numbers to 10, 20, or higher. However, counting objects may be more difficult than reciting numbers and takes practice. Once children understand that counting and quantity are related, they can begin comparing amounts (5 apples are more than 3 apples).

You may notice your child figuring out problems by trial and error, counting lots of things, using a variety of objects to sort and match, drawing patterns, and talking about how she figured out a problem. If you ask her to tell you about the way she sorts, how many objects she has counted, or the pattern the objects form, you'll notice the growth of her ability to explain what she's doing.

FROM SCHOOL TO HOME

Your kindergartner is sure to do a lot of counting in class, whether it's giving napkins and cups to exactly six children at the snack table, singing counting songs, doing counting-finger plays, looking at books that involve counting, or determining the number of wheels on four toy cars. She may also put the numbers in order on a number board or solve simple number problems while playing a computer game.

She'll seek and find plenty of counting and quantifying opportunities at home, too. Cookies taste even better after she's asked for a specific number and then counted them out. And how many numbers will she recite during "Hide and Seek"? She's apt to count almost anything, including the number of stairs as she goes up to bed and the number of family members at the table. She may even figure out whether there are more boys or more girls in the family or compare amounts of food on various plates—"You have more grapes than I do."

It's Your Turn

You can count on your child to count when you:

✦ **Count out loud.** While going about your daily routine, count the plates, forks, and spoons as you set the table, the steps as you take the stairs, the socks as you put them in the washer, and so on. When you do this you help your child learn counting and one-to-one correspondence in a natural way rather than out of context.

✦ **Let her pick fruit,** by counting out the number of apples or oranges you want at the market.

✦ **Solve problems on a plate.** Ask your child, "How many cookies should I put on the plate so that everyone can have two?"

✦ **Cook by the numbers.** How many potatoes will you wash for dinner? Two for Dad and one each for everyone else.

✦ **Dress by the numbers.** Encourage your child to count the buttons on her shirt or sweater as you help her get dressed.

✦ **Pack in the numbers.** Let your child help you figure out how many pairs of socks you must pack to take to Grandma's if you are going to stay for five days.

✦ **Play counting games on car trips:** For example, "How many cows can we count from home to Grandma's house?" or "How many traffic lights are there between home and the store?"

✦ **Pick books with numbers.** Borrow counting books from the library and read them together.

✦ **Count the mail:** Ask, for example, "How many catalogues came today?"

✦ **Sort leaves.** Collect them together on a walk and, at home, divide them into piles of five leaves each.

✦ **Count cards.** Play dice or card games with your child that involve counting, moving a certain number of spaces, or matching numbers of dots on the dice.

✦ **Surf for numbers on the Web.** Download some public-domain computer games from the Internet that will help your child master counting objects and recognizing number symbols.

GEOMETRY, SPATIAL RELATIONS, AND MEASUREMENT

As five-year-olds play with blocks, shape-sorters, pattern blocks, and peg boards, they learn more than just the names of shapes. They also learn which ones roll or can't roll, which make good ramps, and which can be substituted for others. That's geometry. In addition, kindergartners are using words that describe the relationship of one object to another (*behind*, *in front of*, *on top of*, and so on).

A child will learn measurement words and concepts as he plays with blocks (which is larger or smaller, shorter or longer?) or scales and measuring cups (which is heavier or lighter or holds more or less?). By experimenting and exploring with measuring tools, such as rulers, scales, and measuring cups, he gradually learns the meaning of standard units, such as inches, pounds, and cups. A child will have difficulty grasping units of time, such as hours and weeks until he is closer to eight years old. He does, however, understand time in relation to concrete ideas; for example: "We are going to Grandma's after Thanksgiving."

From School to Home

Through classroom activities, such as gluing shapes on a collage, building designs with pattern blocks, and using various beads for stringing, your child learns the names of a variety of shapes. He plays games, such as Lotto or Bingo, that involve matching and naming shapes. His gym time may include obstacle courses that involve spatial challenges—going *under*, *around*, *through* various objects. Class cooking projects teach him about measuring ingredients. Plus, he may learn to measure and chart the growth of a fast-growing plant.

Shapes of objects at home will then elicit comments, such as, "Our plates are round," or, "My bed is a rectangle." Don't be surprised when he brings home and uses measuring words in interesting ways: "The hamster at school weighs 24 inches." He is now relating a variety of positional words to his everyday life: "My back pack is *behind* the door"; "The ball is *underneath* the bed." Charts are the thing now, and he may make one that shows family heights and weights or that tracks the weather by showing the number of snowy, rainy, or sunny days since vacation.

IT'S YOUR TURN

Watch your child learn about shapes as you:

+ **Go on shape searches.** With your child, look for all the shapes (circle, triangle, rectangle, etc.) you can find inside or outside your home.

+ **Do it on road trips, too.** While riding in a bus or car, look for signs of all shapes.

+ **Make cookies together.** Use various-shaped cutters and talk about the names of the shapes you are making (circles, squares, triangles).

+ **Let him shape play dough with those cookie cutters, too.**

+ **Teach table-setting manners.** Help your child learn to set the table by discussing utensil placement: Forks go on the *left* side and knives and spoons on the *right* side of the plate.

+ **Mouth measurement words.** Talk about *teaspoons*, *tablespoons*, *cups*, *half cups*, and so on when letting your child help mix cake or cookie batter.

+ **Measure and pour.** Have your child pour a cup of soap into the washer; let him measure the powder for making a pitcher of lemonade.

+ **Feed the pet—precisely.** Let your child measure out the right amount of food for the fish or the dog.

+ **Direct your child with positional words.** For example, say: "Please put your teddy bear *beside* your chair"; "The dirty dishes go *into* the dishwasher"; "Please bring me the yardstick, it is hanging *inside* the closet *next to* the vacuum cleaner."

+ **Play do-it-yourself "Concentration."** Help your child make up matching cards for "Concentration" using a variety of shapes; then name the shapes when you play.

+ **Play "Tic-Tac-Toe,"** marking the squares with triangles, rectangles, or diamonds in addition to circles and crosses.

+ **Get directional.** As you go to the store, talk to your child about turning *right* or *left*.

+ **Chart those changes.** Keep a growth chart of your child's height and weight, and talk about the changes as he grows.

+ **Measure your space.** Explore the size and shape of things with your child: "I wonder how long our sidewalk is from the door to the street?"; "Let's see how much space the kitchen table would take if we moved it into the other room."

CHAPTER 19

Scientific Thinking

✦

How things grow, why things work the way they do, what properties make things the same or different—these are some of the things budding scientists are learning in kindergarten. In the process, they are beginning to build some invaluable skills, such as observation and discovery, trial and error, fact-finding and experimentation, questioning and logical thinking. For a five-year-old, practicing science expands to include:

> **Observing, investigating,**
> **and questioning**
>
> **Predicting, explaining, and**
> **forming conclusions**

OBSERVING, INVESTIGATING, AND QUESTIONING

Kindergartners are extremely curious and observant. They want to know why things are the way they are, how things work, and what makes things happen. But they need adults to encourage them to use not only their eyes but also their ears, noses, and hands to gather information about the world around them. They enjoy using special science tools, such as magnifying glasses, binoculars, scales, identification books, plastic tubes, and funnels.

A five-year-old scientist must learn how to organize the information she collects as she observes and asks questions. Learning to sort, group, look for patterns, notice similarities and differences, draw what she sees, and describe her observations with words will help a young child turn her explorations into scientific information. She needs help from adults to learn how to ask more specific questions and how to gather more information.

FROM SCHOOL TO HOME

With the help of her teacher, your kindergartner will learn to ask questions before beginning to study a topic: "What do I want to learn about plants [or bears or any other meaningful topic]?" In class she can use magnifying glasses, magnets, scales, and measuring devices to learn even more about what she is studying. She can experiment with and describe her discoveries using tubes, funnels, wheels, and measuring containers at the sand and water tables. After observing a plant's continued growth or a chick hatching from an egg, she can make a series of drawings that show these events. She may have the opportunity to ask a visiting naturalist questions about the hawk he brought to show the class: "How does the hawk use its feet when eating?"

Your child's scientific curiosity will be revealed to you when she shows interest in and talks about a spider web that has appeared overnight, the moss that grows on stones or trees, squirrels playing in the park, or a telephone repair man. She may ask you the names of birds that come to the back-yard feeder, pose a batch of questions when the plumber comes to fix the pipes, or wonder how a chicken grows in an egg as you make an omelet for breakfast.

It's Your Turn

To nurture your child's budding curiosity:

✦ **Spark her senses.** Encourage your child to look at, listen to, smell, and feel things in her environment.

✦ **Play "Guess What I See?"** To help your child understand the functions of all her senses, describe something you are thinking about by using senses other than sight. For example, "I see something that has a sort of soft yet sort of rough texture. It smells a little sweet and fresh, and if I get close to it I might barely hear a breeze moving through it." (It's grass.)

✦ **Give her a glass.** Teach her how to use a magnifying glass to look more closely at a bug, a leaf, or her fingernails.

✦ **Practice attraction.** Show your child how a magnet works by testing it on different materials.

✦ **Explore weighty matters.** Let your child weigh things on a kitchen scale, which will help her to see which things are heavier than others.

✦ **Play with water.** Have your child experiment with tubes and funnels in the bathtub.

✦ **Take a walk in the park,** and talk about what you see, hear, and smell. Look at something you see on your stroll and wonder about it: for instance, how the moss growing on the side of a rock grows there without any soil.

✦ **Search for nature books.** Borrow books that can help your child identify birds, animals, shells, and plants that you have seen on your walks.

✦ **And do some experimental reading, too.** Borrow a book that shows how to do simple experiments at home, and try some of them out with your child.

✦ **Set an interest example.** Ask questions, such as, "Why do you think that happened?" or, "What do you think might happen if ...?" or, "How could we find out if ...?"

✦ **Help your child with her questions.** Encourage her to ask them, and then help her find ways to find accurate answers by suggesting simple studies or experiments.

✦ **Wonder with your child.** Ask questions about what intrigues you, and make your child a partner in your wonder and in discovery. Ask, for example, "What do you suppose makes a rainbow, with all those beautiful colors, appear in the sky?" Then explore with your child how you both can find the answers.

PREDICTING, EXPLAINING, AND FORMING CONCLUSIONS

The result of young children's eagerness to observe and explore is that they are quick to answer their own questions, form their own opinions, and make predictions. Yet kindergartners often don't have enough information or experience to make realistic or scientifically correct predictions or guesses. That's why they need help in learning how to base their explanations and conclusions on things they've seen (observation), done (experimentation), or learned from a book (research).

FROM SCHOOL TO HOME

Your child's kindergarten teacher knows that the right questions—such as, "Which food do you think the guinea pig will eat if we give him both carrot peels and apple skins to choose from?"—will elicit thoughtful guesses or predictions from him. Similarly, various objects in a tub of water will prompt your five-year-old to explore and predict which things sink and which float. He may keep track on a chart, trying to figure out what makes something sink or float. When he guesses that "heavy things sink and light things float," the teacher can help him evaluate his conclusion by using a scale to see if his explanation is correct. More classroom science: Your child may build a ramp in the block area to use as a race track for cars and learn why the ramp makes cars go faster; the class could observe the rain falling outside and talk about what might happen if the sun comes out while it is still raining.

On his own at home, your curious kindergartner might make rather inaccurate statements of fact, such as, "I know why the shell makes a noise when you put it up to your ear; it's because there is a bug living in there." Or he might come up with a "kidsensical" interpretation of why the toaster isn't toasting right. These observations show that he's trying to make sense of the world—relating conclusions to things he already knows or has experienced. For example, he may guess that your pet is shedding hair all over the furniture because "maybe Brownie is getting ready for summer"; his explanation of why it's dark out might be "because the sun is on the other side of the world." Previous exploration may have him guessing that the seeds planted in the garden will be showing tomorrow.

IT'S YOUR TURN

To encourage scientific exploration:

+ **Grow things together.** Plant a vegetable garden or a window flower box. Guess with your child which seeds will sprout first; then keep track to see if your guesses were right.

+ **...and plant a carrot top or an avocado pit.** Guess how long it will take to sprout, and keep a chart of the growth of stems and leaves.

+ **Question his conclusions.** Respond to your child's explanations by asking, "How do you know that?" or, "Tell me why you think that." This will encourage him to organize the information that fuels his findings.

+ **Offer concise answers.** Try to give your child short and simple explanations when he asks about how something works. Be accurate, but try not to make it too complicated.

+ **...and tell others to do it, too.** Encourage people, such as your doctor, veterinarian, plumber, or electrician, to give your child explanations to his questions that he can understand.

+ **Show him how you conclude.** Set an example for your child by telling him how you came up with your explanations and conclusions.

+ **Explore the unexpected.** Talk with your child about unusual things, such as what makes a rainbow, why elephants don't live in the United States, and so on.

+ **Track the weather.** Keep a chart together, making guesses about how cold it is by noticing frost, frozen puddles, and clouds covering the sun before looking at the thermometer.

+ **Track tracks.** If you see animal tracks in the snow or muddy paw prints on the hood of your car, guess which animal might have made them; then look in a book together to see if you are right.

+ **Find answers in books.** Borrow age-appropriate books from the library that explain how things work or that answer the questions your child is wondering about. Also, find books about things you would like your child to learn more about, such as how birds build nests or how some birds know to fly away from the cold and where to go for the winter.

CHAPTER 20

Social Studies

✦

Young children want and need to learn about people and places, the way we all live together and influence each other, the reasons we need to agree about how to live together, and how we affect our world. In kindergarten, children learn about these subjects by looking at themselves, their families, their homes, and their communities. For five-year-olds, social studies concerns:

People and how they live together

**How the past, the land, and people
affect one another**

PEOPLE AND HOW THEY LIVE TOGETHER

Depending on their life experiences, kindergartners may or may not be comfortable around people who are different from themselves. They may not know much about ways of living that are different from their own. Five-year-olds are just beginning to realize that people depend upon one another to live their lives. They are exploring family roles and the ways in which community helpers are essential to our health and safety.

At this age your child is beginning to understand why rules are necessary for people to coexist. She is aware of leaders and why we need to have skilled and helpful people in charge of groups and activities. She and her peers take comfort in clear rules that are consistently followed.

FROM SCHOOL TO HOME

In school your five-year-old takes part in discussions about the ways everyone in the class is the same and also about the ways each is different from one another. She has the opportunity to talk and read about different kinds of families that vary in size, way of life, type of home, and way of earning money. Class trips to a variety of workplaces in the community help your child understand what different jobs are about. Safety walks help her learn about traffic signs, stop lights, police officers, road lines, and other neighborhood essentials. She may ask questions and then draw pictures to show what she has learned. Plus, she can explore the intriguing community of the World Wide Web on the classroom computer.

Then she'll come home and comment about how different workers in the community do things to help people: "The veterinarian takes care of animals"; "The mail carrier delivers letters." On a walk with you she may stare at and ask you questions about people who look different; or she may ask about the rules of traffic safety and wonder how everyone knows those rules. Notice her curiosity about television shows or books that have different kinds of people in them. And don't be surprised when she asks, "Who is the boss of the family?" or, "Who is the boss of the world?"

IT'S YOUR TURN

To help your child understand others:

+ **Give a straight answer.** Respond honestly and simply to her questions about people and their differences.

+ **Diversify her social circle.** Help your child meet people from a variety of backgrounds.

+ **Enjoy variety.** Set an example for your child by appreciating people's differences.

+ **Visit a healthcare facility.** Take your child to a nursing home and help her talk to the people who live there. Appreciating older citizens is another way to appreciate the world.

+ **Encourage inclusion.** To help your child respect and embrace differences in people, suggest that she have playdates in your home with children of varying lifestyles and backgrounds, including those with special needs.

+ **Talk about your family.** Discuss the similarities of and differences in your ages, size, hair and eye color, and talents (ability to work on cars or motorcycles, sing, draw, garden, do plumbing, and so on). Chat about how your family works together, and make a family job chart that shows what each member does to help others in the family.

+ **...and about who's in charge.** Discuss what it might be like if parents weren't in charge of children and what she likes about living in a family with parents who are in charge.

+ **Show her that rules vary.** Talk about how rules of behavior are different in different places. For example, rules about riding in your own car are different from rules about riding in a bus or subway. Rules at home are different from rules at a friend's house, at Grandma's house, or at school.

+ **Point out the community around you.** Talk about others who help your family, such as the building superintendent, people in the electric power company, the garbage collector, the school custodian, the principal, the food-store clerks, the librarian, and so on.

+ **Bolster her book list.** Read books about many kinds of people, including those of varying racial and ethnic backgrounds.

+ **Play games and learn the rules.** Discuss why there must be rules and how the game could not be played if everyone made up her own rules.

+ **Stop, go, walk, and wait.** Point out to your child the various traffic rules, and discuss what would happen if these rules were not obeyed.

HOW THE PAST, THE LAND, AND PEOPLE AFFECT ONE ANOTHER

Kindergartners are just beginning to appreciate the importance of caring for the land, water, and air around them. They can understand that if there are empty bottles along the road or gasoline spills floating on the water, people are the ones who made this happen. Helping to take care of the land and the water makes them feel important and useful.

Five-year-olds are also developing a sense of the geography of their environment. They think more about what their environment looks like in terms of taking care of it and representing it spatially in simple maps. They learn to describe their environment—both the beauty of it and the misuse of it—by drawing pictures and making models.

FROM SCHOOL TO HOME

School is a great place to nurture a child's awareness of the environment. Your child may take part in classroom or school recycling projects, as well as sing songs, read books, and listen to poems about keeping the environment clean. He also learns about his relationship to the places and people around him and may draw maps of the classroom, the playground, or his bedroom to explore this concept. After a class walk around the neighborhood, his teacher may encourage him to make a list of what he saw and then build a model of it in the block area. He is now able to think about why being near a river enables his community to do certain things and to imagine what it would be like to live far away from a river or other water.

Your child may come home eager to describe what he's seen on the bus to and from school. In your neighborhood your child may notice and comment on trash by the road as you drive or walk by. Next time out he'll want to take a trash bag so he can pick up litter left by others.

IT'S YOUR TURN

To encourage your child's environmental awareness:

✦ **Take walks.** Notice details that are specific to your neighborhood and environment, such as tall buildings, wild-growing plants, or public transportation.

✦ **Discuss decor.** Point out to your child how people have made their surroundings special with gardens, bushes, fences, and trees.

✦ **Talk trash.** Discuss what it would be like if everyone threw their trash on the ground instead of taking it to a waste bin.

✦ **Teach him how you reduce, re-use, and recycle trash.** And talk with your child about why you need to recycle or fix things that break rather than throwing them away.

✦ **Make maps.** Help him begin to understand geography and mapping by drawing simple treasure maps or scavenger-hunt maps for him to follow around your home or yard.

✦ **Draw your neighborhood.** Help your child make drawings of the part of the city or town where you live.

✦ **Build yourselves a house:** Make a model with blocks or Legos, creating together the basic way your house or apartment building looks from the outside.

✦ **Chat about climate control.** Talk with your child about how your climate affects your life and why you use storm windows, screens, air conditioners, and fans.

✦ **Read about other towns.** Find books on cities or towns in other parts of the country, and discuss how it would affect what you do for fun if you lived near a big lake or the ocean or what it would be like if you lived near a mountain.

✦ **...and other countries.** Read stories to your child about children living in warm countries, such as Mexico, or cold countries, such as Iceland; discuss how temperature affects the way people live, what they do for fun, the kinds of clothes they wear, and the kinds of houses in which they live.

CHAPTER 21

The Arts

◆

All children are artists—people who find creative ways to express and share their ideas, thoughts, and feelings. When children create with crayons, paint, clay, blocks, or even a pile of recycled materials, they are artists. When they put on a skit or a puppet show, make up a song, or dance to music, they are artists. Five-year-olds are also learning to understand and appreciate the artistic work of other people. Children learn about the arts through:

Artistic expression

Artistic appreciation

ARTISTIC EXPRESSION

Kindergartners have lots of ideas and knowledge in their heads. Although they may not be able to tell you in words about all of their thoughts, they might be able to show you a lot about what they are thinking and feeling if they are given a chance to be creative. They paint or draw pictures, make sculptures, build roads and buildings, make up songs and dances, and put on puppet shows. Not every five-year-old will be comfortable with all of these artistic forms, but they all love to create in some way.

Your child may be a builder but not a singer, a dancer but not a painter, or a sculptor but not an actor. It's important to encourage and support your child's individual modes of creativity and avenues of artistic expression, not only to promote your child's special skills and interests, but also because creativity positively affects many other areas of learning.

FROM SCHOOL TO HOME

The kindergarten classroom is a mecca for creative expression. Your child is encouraged to use her talents in all kinds of ways: She can work with a variety of art materials to depict a story or to show what she learned on a field trip or how she solved a math problem. She might act out a character from a story. She might use musical instruments for sound effects in a puppet show or as an accompaniment when singing a song. Music inspires her to move and dance to different rhythms or to express different moods. And blocks, Legos, or recycled objects are there for her to craft inventions, build towns, make machines, and construct houses.

Then your child brings her stimulated imagination home. She paints and draws. She sings songs as she goes about daily activities and claps her hands to music. You may see her pretend to be a nurse, a police officer, a teacher, or a store clerk. And don't be surprised if she uses a puppet or imaginary friend to express her thoughts and emotions.

"I particularly like the arts section, because it shows how art can be found and practiced in everyday settings."

It's Your Turn

To encourage and promote your child's creative instincts:

✦ **Sing to her**—while riding in the car, while giving her a bath, or while she gets dressed.

✦ **Write the songs together.** Make up songs that rhyme or that tell a story about an adventure you and she shared.

✦ **Get the beat.** Clap your hands, stamp your feet, or dance with your child to the rhythm of music.

✦ **Make an instrument.** Teach your child how to make and use simple musical instruments, such as a drum made from an oatmeal container or coffee can or a kazoo made by wrapping tissue around a comb.

✦ **Keep art supplies on hand**—crayons, markers, and paper—to encourage your child to express her ideas and feelings in creative ways.

✦ **Foster her originality.** Help your child fulfill her creative urge by supplying her with everyday items—different-sized boxes, glue, tape, a stapler, paper bags, scraps, buttons, bread tags—that might inspire her to create something unique.

✦ **Talk art.** Encourage your child to talk about her creations by saying, "Tell me about your picture," or asking, "What were you thinking about while you were dancing?"

✦ **Be her audience**—when she dances, puts on skits, or performs in any way.

✦ **Let her build.** Give your child building materials, such as blocks, construction toys, or empty boxes.

✦ **Put on a puppet show.** Provide a few finger or hand puppets, and help your child tell stories with them; encourage her to express her thoughts or feelings by having the puppets talk for her.

✦ **Start from scratch.** Make homemade play dough together; then use it to sculpt animals, a house, a tree, flowers.

✦ **Inspire art with art.** Together, make finger paint out of shaving cream and food color. Then paint creatively while listening to different kinds of music.

✦ **Put the icing on the cake.** Encourage your child to decorate a birthday cake for someone in the family.

ARTISTIC APPRECIATION

Even if your kindergartner is not a painter, dancer, or musician, he can still love the arts. Five-year-olds are beginning to have opinions about the artwork or performances. They can learn to enjoy listening to music, watching plays or puppet shows, and looking at paintings, drawings, and sculptures created by others. And art stimulates their natural curiosity: Kindergartners are interested in how artists create certain effects.

FROM SCHOOL TO HOME

The arts are an ongoing commodity in a kindergarten classroom. Your child watches classmates perform a puppet show or a dance they have created and asks questions or makes helpful comments about the performance. He also listens to music during choice time and moves to the rhythms. Visiting poets, musicians, or actors may inspire him to draw a picture afterwards as a way of saying thank you. He has opportunities to go to the library to look for books illustrated by a particular artist. And at this age he can begin to appreciate the role of a conductor leading an orchestra.

At home your five-year-old will comment about the illustrations in a book or in a magazine and explain why he likes them. He is more selective about music and will turn up the radio when a favorite song or musical piece comes on. Now he can appreciate a sibling's music concert, dance show, or school play and offer a compliment. He's curious about how art happens and will ask about how a TV cartoon, a town statue, or a sculpture in a museum is made.

"These ideas are not only educational, they help me and my child stay close. And they're fun to do!"

IT'S YOUR TURN

To train your young art enthusiast:

✦ **Discuss what you see.** Encourage your child to talk about the work of artists by asking him questions: "How do you think the movie makers made that happen?"; "Which instruments do you like the best in that music?"; "What does that painting make you think about?"

✦ **Play a variety of recorded music.** Let your child become familiar with many sounds, and help him hear the differences and similarities among varying styles of music.

✦ **Get emotional.** Talk about how each of you feels when you listen to different kinds of music.

✦ **Don't forget kid music.** Enjoy your child's appreciation of music performed by artists such as Ella Jenkins, Raffi, or the cast of *Sesame Street*.

✦ **Focus on the pictures.** Talk about the illustrations in books as you read to your child.

✦ **Museum-hop.** Take your child to museums for short periods of time, talk about what he likes, and, perhaps, ask questions of the museum staff.

✦ **See a show.** Try to attend live performances when possible: a puppet show, a magic act, a circus, a musical fairy tale, a children's concert, a ballet.

✦ **Note those notes.** Stop and listen to a musician playing in the mall or on the street.

✦ **Appreciate craft.** Stop and watch the person sewing names on caps or shirts at a street-fair booth or in a store display.

✦ **Admire the architecture.** Point out interesting buildings in the city, and talk with your child about who might have designed a building that tall and what he or she must have known in order to plan it.

CHAPTER 22

Physical Development and Health

◆

Children learn by doing, and at this age so much of what they do is highly active and physical. It follows, then, that children's physical development and the health of their bodies are very important to their mental development. Opportunities to use and develop their bodies help kindergartners think, reason, and learn well. Plus, their confidence grows as they master motor skills—confidence that helps them to be successful learners. We look at children's physical development in three areas:

Large-muscle development

Small-muscle development

Personal health and safety

LARGE-MUSCLE DEVELOPMENT

Kindergartners are on the move; they never seem to stop. Whether running, jumping, spinning, climbing, or dancing, they are eager to do things fast and are always busy practicing different movements and trying out new ways of using their bodies. They love physical challenges!

FROM SCHOOL TO HOME

School offers five-year-olds ample opportunities for movement. Your kindergartner spends time outside or in the gym running, climbing, jumping, and swinging. With her teacher and peers she plays ball games that involve throwing and catching. She may also practice special motor skills, such as walking forward, sideways, and backward on a balance beam. She is offered many occasions to move in different ways—gallop, walk, skip, hop. In addition, she learns to loosen and relax her body through stretching exercises.

Your child will find plenty of chances to use her large-motor skills at home. She may carry bulky objects up and down stairs or carry food and drinks to the table without spilling. Increasing strength will enable her to move large boxes or carry a heavier bundle than she could before. You'll see her play highly active games with siblings and friends. And get ready: She may be ready to learn to ride a two-wheeler without training wheels.

IT'S YOUR TURN

Boost your child's physical abilities when you:

✦ **Give her room to move.** Encourage active play every day in the neighborhood, your yard, or in an organized sports program.

✦ **Jump together.** Try jumping rope with her, fast or slow, moving forward or standing in place.

✦ **Play ball!** Throw and catch together, maybe using a mitt; practice batting, too.

✦ **Get out the bikes.** Go on short bike rides with your child, and maybe plan to cycle to a special park for a weekend picnic.

✦ **Go for strolls.** Take evening walks with your child on a regular schedule.

✦ **Challenge her.** Encourage your child to try to reach new physical goals, such as hopping on one foot 50 times, leaping over big boxes, walking up the stairs backwards, and so on.

✦ **Let her help you with physical chores.** Ask your child to take out the trash or vacuum the rug. And encourage her to help with outside work, such as raking leaves or shoveling snow.

✦ **Shoot hoops.** Set up a lower-than-standard-height basketball hoop and practice throwing baskets together.

✦ **Send her out to play.** Encourage your child to play outside in the fresh air and open space. If possible, set up a swing set or rope-and-tire swing in your yard; or fashion a climbing-bar maze or a balance beam to offer her playtime challenges.

✦ **Hit the park.** Occasionally walk to a nearby park or playground with your child so she can run, jump, and climb on the equipment.

✦ **Share sports.** Engage in activities you both enjoy, such as swimming, Rollerblading, or ice skating.

✦ **Dance with props.** Use paper streamers or silk scarves to inspire both of you to move creatively.

✦ **Look for movement opportunities.** For example, walk up the stairs at the department store instead of using the elevator or escalator.

SMALL-MUSCLE DEVELOPMENT

Kindergartners develop increased dexterity as they use the small muscles of their hands and fingers. They are now able to manage tasks—tying shoes, cutting up food, or pouring milk—that would have been too difficult for them at age four. (Remember, some five-year-olds may have difficulty with these tasks, as there is a wide range of skill level among children of this age.) More and more they enjoy working puzzles, building things with small pieces, and completing craft projects. And it's now easier for them to use pencils, pens, and markers.

FROM SCHOOL TO HOME

The kindergarten class offers many opportunities for small-motor activity. Your child uses a variety of hand tools, such as scissors, a stapler, a staple remover, a tape dispenser, and a hole-puncher to craft and create things. He probably draws and writes every day, using pencils, pens, markers, typewriters, and perhaps a computer. He builds and makes things with his hands, using beads, recycled materials, string, Legos, and pattern blocks, and he creates increasingly more intricate patterns and structures with these items. Your five-year-old now spends more and more time doing small-muscle activities that require planning and result in an end product. This goes beyond the more simple exploration of materials he was doing a year ago.

He'll use his new-found dexterity buttoning his shirt, zipping his jacket, and tying his shoes while getting dressed at home. Notice, too, that he builds bigger, more complicated structures with his Legos, Tinkertoys, Lincoln Logs, or table blocks than he did last year. He can also put together jigsaw puzzles with smaller and more numerous pieces. Your child uses writing tools more consistently and for longer periods of time and now asks to use scissors to cut out pictures from a magazine.

IT'S YOUR TURN

To teach those busy little fingers:

✦ **Let him dress himself,** and encourage your child to button his buttons and practice tying his shoes.

✦ **Give him good jobs.** Ask him to do chores involving small-motor skills, such as setting the table, pouring his milk, or peeling vegetables.

✦ **Work with tools.** Teach your child how to do simple carpentry tasks by working on things he enjoys, such as making a bird feeder to put outside the window.

✦ **Bring out the chef in him.** Cook together: For example, make scrambled eggs and let him crack open the eggs and mix them with a fork or whisk.

✦ **...or the tailor in him.** Do some simple sewing projects together: Stitch around two squares of cloth to make a stuffed pillow for his bed, or work on a costume for Halloween.

✦ **Inspire your child to write or draw.** Each day suggest various topics, such as drawing what he dreamed about last night, "writing" a letter to Grandma telling her about the flowers in the yard, or drawing pictures of his family or favorite toys.

✦ **String beads together.**

✦ **Create designs with pegs and boards.**

✦ **Construct with paper.** Make designs with cut-out colored pieces of paper.

✦ **...and with Legos.** Encourage him to build specific structures, such as a bridge or a barn.

✦ **Make little people.** Together, create your own paper people by cutting out images from magazines and then drawing and cutting out clothes for them.

✦ **Play cards.** Try games, such as "Concentration," in which he has to pick up and turn over cards, or "Old Maid" or "Go Fish," in which he must hold cards in his hand and place cards on the table in piles.

✦ **Work trickier puzzles.** Find some jigsaw puzzles with smaller pieces than he is accustomed to, and encourage him to fit the pieces together himself.

PERSONAL HEALTH AND SAFETY

Kindergartners are able to take care of many of their own physical needs, such as toileting, dressing, and brushing their teeth. They are also increasingly aware of health and safety issues, such as traffic dangers, fire hazards, sickness, and unhealthy foods. Children of this age are eager to care for themselves and be responsible about safety on their own, but they need help, support, and reminders.

From School to Home

The kindergarten teacher offers five-year-olds plenty of ways to take care of themselves. Your child keeps track of her own belongings by putting them into a cubby or her knapsack. She is urged to clean up after spills and messy projects and to wash her hands before eating or participating in class cooking projects. She may also take part in discussions and role plays about health and nutrition, fire safety, or traffic rules and procedures.

At home your child is able to take care of her toileting needs independently, wash her own hands and face, and brush her teeth and hair with little or no help. And all your talk about eating healthy foods has paid off: She will now tell the family why it is important to drink milk or water several times every day or ask if a fruit and a vegetable are included in this meal. She knows to proceed with care around the kitchen stove, the heater, or electrical appliances. And she may tell a younger sibling to be careful near the street.

"These examples are great because they show that you can give children responsibility while still expressing love and affection."

IT'S YOUR TURN

To help keep your child healthy and safe:

✦ **Encourage her to handle self-care.** Talk about good health practices, such as always washing hands after using the bathroom or before eating; demonstrate that you do this yourself; and praise her ability to take care of her own hygiene.

✦ **Teach brushing by example.** Help her learn to brush her teeth correctly by brushing at the same time she does so she can see how you brush and for how long.

✦ **Teach sneezing etiquette.** Help your child use common-courtesy health rules, such as covering her mouth when she coughs or sneezes and throwing away soiled tissues in a wastebasket.

✦ **Talk nutrition.** Explain why you serve certain foods and not others, that the foods help people to grow and be healthy as well as taste good. In this way you'll help her see that nutrition and taste are both important to good eating.

✦ **And talk about meal planning.** Discuss the menus you plan and why you choose the foods you do—why you serve vegetables with dinner, have whole-grain bread, include a glass of milk, and so on. Don't forget to focus on the aesthetics, too, such as why you have certain colors of foods on the dinner plate and how the flavors complement one another.

✦ **Always be firm about street-safety rules.** In addition, when you teach your child the rules about crossing the street, encourage her to be the one who tells you when it is safe to cross.

✦ **...and car safety rules.** When riding in the car, be very clear about wearing a seat belt, when it is safe to open the door, to wait for you after getting out and closing the car door, and so on.

✦ **Demonstrate safe driving practices,** and tell your child when and why you are observing a safety procedure.

✦ **Focus on bike safety too.** Teach your child safety procedures, such as always wearing a helmet, knowing the boundaries for where she can ride, and so on.

✦ **Stage fire drills.** Plan a fire-evacuation procedure with the family, and then practice every six months or so.

Looking Ahead

◆

As this book ends, your child is looking forward eagerly to first grade—to new subjects to learn, new discoveries to make, and new friends to meet. Because of your involvement, your child knows that learning does not stop at the classroom door. His family creates a learning environment at home where he, and everyone in the family, continues to learn every day.

Parents are a child's first teacher. We hope that this book has helped you turn everyday activities into enjoyable discoveries that add to your child's store of knowledge, challenge her imagination, and build her character.

Learning, for your child and yourself, is what it should be—a rich and rewarding part of daily life.

Along the way, we hope that you have discovered a great deal about your child's unique gifts, interests, and talents, and that you have found countless ways to nurture them. We have tried to help you come up with inventive ways to build interest and skills that will give your child an extra boost.

We encourage you to continue this approach so that the bridge between home and school remains strong. Many of the activities you share with your child in the years and months ahead may not be new—they may just be variations of what you are currently doing. But today's favorites can spark new ideas. Be open to them and enjoy learning and discovering with your child.

Over time, your child will also be able to participate increasingly in some of your own hobbies and favorite pastimes. These make for great learning opportunities. They also help you build shared interests and form close bonds with your child.

Children's pride and joy in themselves knows no bounds when they make a new discovery or master a new skill. By continuing to use the activities and approach of this book, you are helping to create countless numbers of such "winning" situations. These experiences are invaluable for your child, and they are rewarding and fun for you and everyone else involved.

Keep on with the good practices you have set in place and the relationship you are continuing to strengthen. You are building a strong foundation for your child's life and learning. And you are creating priceless memories for the years to come.

Our best wishes to you and your family,

Sam Meisels, Dot Marsden, and Charlotte Stetson

About the Authors

Samuel J. Meisels, Ed.D., is a professor of education and a research scientist at the University of Michigan. He is widely regarded as the nation's leading authority on the assessment of young children. He has pioneered the development of alternative assessment strategies, including the *Work Sampling System®* on which *Winning Ways to Learn* is based. These strategies have been used successfully by tens of thousands of teachers nationwide for over a decade to keep track of how children learn and develop. Because of their effectiveness in assisting teachers  and in measuring achievement, these strategies are now mandated for young children in a number of states throughout the country.

Major areas of Dr. Meisels's professional commitment include: *developing alternative assessment strategies; the impact of standardized tests on young children; early identification of disability and risk conditions in early childhood; and developmental consequences of high-risk birth.*

Dr. Meisels has published more than 100 articles, books, and monographs in the fields of early childhood development and education, assessment, and special education. He serves as a consultant to numerous state departments of education, government agencies, private research institutes, and foundations. He is the president-elect of the Board of Zero to Three: The National Center for Infants, Toddlers and Families and has held senior advisory positions with many organizations including Head Start and the National Academy of Sciences.

Dorothea B. Marsden, M.Ed., is a nationally known early childhood educator, trainer, and developer of assessments for preschoolers and school-age children. She has helped design and direct numerous innovative, high-quality early childhood programs in Massachusetts and Vermont. She is a consultant to the national Early Head Start program and was one of the primary authors and professional developers for the *Work Sampling System*®. She is the co-author of the *Early Screening Inventory-Revised*® and additional assessment materials.

Charlotte Stetson, M.Ed., is a leading developer of educational programs for young children, and has worked extensively with teachers on developmentally-appropriate curriculum, instruction, and assessment. A former first- and second-grade teacher, she is a contributing author to the teaching materials for the *Work Sampling System*®. She has co-authored books for teachers about curriculum development and is the author of a book for parents designed to help their children learn math skills, entitled *You Can Count on Mother Goose*.

About the
Work Sampling System®

✦

The *Work Sampling System*® is an authentic performance assessment that provides an alternative to group-administered, norm-referenced achievement tests in preschool through fifth grade. Its purpose is to document and assess children's skills, knowledge, behavior, and accomplishments across a wide variety of curriculum areas on multiple occasions.

The *Work Sampling System* consists of three complementary elements:

1) Development Guidelines and Checklists

2) Portfolios of Children's Work

3) Summary Reports

Assessments based on the *Work Sampling* approach take place three times a year. They are designed to reflect classroom goals and objectives and to help teachers keep track of children's continuous progress by placing their work within a broad, developmental perspective. Through its focus on documenting individual performance of classroom-based tasks, *Work Sampling* enhances student motivation, assists teachers in instructional decision-making, and serves as an effective means for reporting children's progress to families, professional educators, and the community.

For more information, please call (800) 435-3085
or access www.rebusinc.com.

Also from Goddard Press

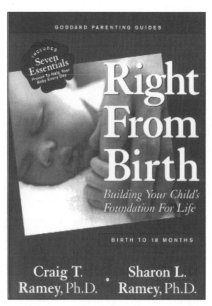

Right From Birth: Building Your Child's Foundation for Life—Birth to 18 Months, by Craig T. Ramey, PhD and Sharon L. Ramey, PhD. $24.95 cloth, $19.95 paperback

An authoritative, up-to-the-minute guide on early learning, communication, social skills, and emotional growth in infancy.

Gold Award Winner from the National Parenting Publications Awards Council—"...a calm, clearly written discussion of how to build a better baby."

A 1999 Parents Choice Award winner—"A helpful breakdown of the most important developmental aspects of each growth stage."

Me, Myself and I: How Children Build Their Sense of Self—18 to 36 Months, by Kyle D. Pruett, MD. $24.95 cloth, $19.95 paperback

A definitive guide to toddlerhood—the extraordinary period when parents and caregivers have the greatest influence in setting a child on a healthy and happy course for life.

Gold Award Winner from the National Parenting Publications Awards Council—"A fine overview of these challenging years."

On *CHILD* Magazine's 1999 list, "Best Parenthood Books of the Year."

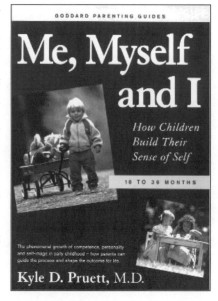

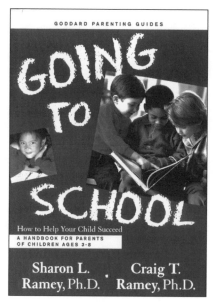

Going to School: How to Help Your Child Succeed—A Handbook for Parents of Children Ages 3 to 8, by Sharon L. Ramey, PhD and Craig T. Ramey, PhD. $19.95 paperback

A landmark resource filled with proven strategies for preparing children to start school and to helping them succeed in the critical early years.

"Abundant advice and hand-holding in this sensible guide." *Publishers Weekly*

A 1999 Parents Choice Award winner— "This thorough guide ... explains how families can help ease the transition into school and participate actively in their kids' education."

✦ ✦ ✦ ✦

Winning Ways to Learn: Ages 6, 7 & 8—600 Great Ideas to Help Children by Samuel J. Meisels, Ed.D., Charlotte Stetson, M.Ed., and Dorothea B. Marsden, M.Ed. $15.95 paperback

A "home" version of a renowned, proven approach to boosting children's school readiness and early school performance.

"...a comprehensive and humane set of activities suitable for young children everywhere."
Howard Gardner, author of *Frames of Mind: The Theory of Multiple Intelligences*

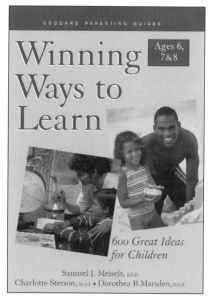